VIRGINS

Redefining SINGLE Sexuality

Doug Rosenau, Ed.D.
Michael Todd Wilson, M.S.

Sexual
Wholeness
Resources
Atlanta, GA

Published by Sexual Wholeness Resources, Atlanta, GA.

Originally published in paperback by Baker Books

ISBN: 978-0-9858107-1-9 (Paperback)

ISBN: 978-0-9858107-0-2 (eBook version)

Recommended Catalog information:

Rosenau, Doug.

Soul virgins : redefining single sexuality / Douglas Rosenau, Michael Todd Wilson.

Includes bibliographical references.

1. Single people—Religious life. 2. Single people—Sexual behavior. 3. Sex—Religious aspects—Christianity. 4. Chastity. I. Wilson, Michael Todd. II. Title.

BV4596.S5R67

241.66—dc22

Front cover by graphicN3 designs.

Cover images © 2012 - Liv friis-larsen (top) & Galyna Andrushko (bottom). Used under license from Shutterstock.com.

To Michael Todd and my daughter Merrill's generation:

Please forgive my generation:

> for abandoning you to a sexual revolution that created such ungodly directions,

> for not challenging more bravely our sexually obsessed and confused culture,

> for not initiating wise dialogue that would have produced better answers,

> for not taking the time to help you understand and reject terribly distorted values, and

> for not encouraging you to courageously fight through to a godly understanding of sexual wholeness that truly works.

Doug

To Doug and his fellow baby boomers:

We forgive your generation, for yours was the first in American history to grow up without Scripture as its firm moral compass.

Your misdirection and neglect are no excuse for our irresponsibility.

It's not too late to build a bridge together that will rise above the sexual confusion of our culture and make a lasting difference, not only for our generation but also for that of our children and your grandchildren.

Let's together help my generation build a godly sexual attitude that pursues true intimacy at the heart of God's sexual economy.

Michael Todd

Contents

Definitions and Models

Before you begin the soul virgin journey, you will want to become familiar with a few of our terms and definitions, since we may use some words in ways you aren't used to. You will want to refer to these two pages often, especially with regard to the new models presented here.

Soul Virgin: A *soul virgin* is one who continuously seeks to value, celebrate, and protect God's design for sexuality—body, soul, and spirit—in oneself and others.

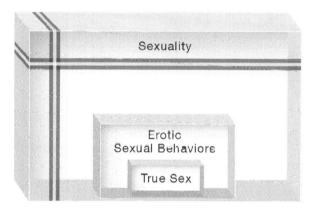

Sexuality: What we experience relationally in our day-to-day interactions with others. Our sexuality propels each of us to desire genuine relational connection with God, others, and a potential mate. Sexuality also includes our general sexual desire and gender makeup, masculine and feminine. This is the large box we *all* live in—whether we want to admit it or not—because we *are* all sexual beings.

Erotic Sexual Behaviors: These are actions (both physical and mental) that are romantic or erotically arousing, such as fantasy, sex talk, kissing, and caressing.

True Sex: Those most intimate of erotic sexual behaviors that are biblically reserved for marriage between man and woman (Hebrews 13:4). At minimum, "true sex" includes all intercourse behavior (oral, anal, vaginal) and mutual orgasms. However, true sex may include other erotic sexual behaviors as well—especially those including genital expression.

The Relationship Continuum Bridge

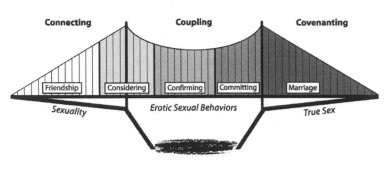

Connecting: The type of relationship we have with most people—same-sex and opposite-sex friendship. Connecting also includes two people who have gone on any number of dates but have yet to define themselves as a couple deliberately evaluating marriage. Sexuality may be fully enjoyed in these relationships; however, there is no place for *any* erotic sexual behaviors (including true sex) in connecting relationships.

Coupling: Only a small number of relationships in a person's lifetime will begin the journey across the Bridge. These are man and woman relationships who have likely been on a number of dates and, as a result, desire to intentionally explore the possibility of future marriage. Coupling includes the ideas of exclusivity, romance, and dedication to the process of moving down the continuum toward Covenanting (marriage). Erotic sexual behaviors are negotiated by the couple based on their unique relationship, with true sex biblically reserved for marriage. There are three distinct stages in Coupling:

Considering: This initial stage most often begins while still as a connecting relationship. Yet once they define the relationship as a couple (Coupling), they dedicate themselves to the process of prayerfully considering whether the other is what they truly seek in a soul mate.

Confirming: Sometimes called "engaged to be engaged." A couple seeks premarital counseling and sets aside time for full disclosure of each other's past. This allows the couple time to work through real issues *prior to* the emotional and social pressures of formal engagement.

Committing: This is engagement. The couple following our model may enjoy a relatively short committing stage— long enough to complete the practical matters of wedding and honeymoon planning and the merging of two separate lives.

Covenanting: This covenant relationship of marriage occurs with the official "I do" in the presence of loved ones who pledge to hold the new husband and wife accountable to their lifelong commitment to each other. In this relationship, true sex may be enjoyed without guilt and with God's full blessing.

Acknowledgments

Thank you, team! Four people especially helped us in the writing of various parts of this book (their contributions are acknowledged in the chapters on which they collaborated with us). Together we spent many hours creating ideas, developing language, and polishing content. A special thanks to:

Vickie George, a competent and gifted marriage counselor and sex therapist. She is also a colleague of Doug and Michael Todd at the Intimacy Counseling Center. Vickie was single until age thirty and single-again for ten years until she met the love of her life, Wayne.

Erica Tan, a never-married single adult who recently completed her doctorate in psychology from Regent University. Erica is also a competent researcher and author and lives in Virginia Beach, Virginia.

Anna Maya, a never-married single adult living in the Orlando area. She is a creative and intuitive therapist working with adolescents at the University Behavioral Center in Orlando, Florida.

David Hall, a never-married single adult completing his master's practicum at the Psychological Studies Institute in Atlanta, Georgia. He is also a talented writer and creative communicator.

Other heartfelt thank-yous go to:

Doug's wife, Catherine, who deserves much gratitude for sacrificing her love language of quality time together to support his time-consuming writing schedule. Without her, his books would never be written.

Some of Michael Todd's "inner circle" of friends—especially Jace Broadhurst, Sherry Gardener, and Melissa Copeland—who through the years have served as faithful sounding boards on many of the concepts contained in this book.

Michael Todd's parents and grandparents, whose undying dedication to his life and ministry have been a never-ending source of encouragement.

Others passionate about single sexuality issues who provided review for our manuscript, including Tanya Foster, Phillips Hwang, Christine McDaniels, Josh McGinnis, Erin Merrion, Julie Rosenau, Brandon Santan, Bridgett Sullivan, Michael Sytsma, Debra Taylor, and Lorraine Turbyfill.

The folks at Baker Publishing Group for taking the risk with us to create a much-needed dialogue to influence a generation of single adults back toward the Father's heart, especially our editors, Vicki Crumpton, Kristin Kornoelje, and Brian Peterson.

And lastly, our heavenly Father, from whom and through whom and to whom are all things—soul virgins included.

Introduction

Principle:
Wise readers never skip introductions!

God deliberately created you with a unique sexual identity. You were created as a one-of-a-kind sexual being, making you a man or woman with alluring power, erotic desire, and gender attitudes all your own. Your sexuality gives you the awesome ability to experience intimate closeness in relationships. Living according to God's blueprint for sexuality empowers you to enjoy a true celebration of intimacy.

Unfortunately, sexuality isn't always seen as such a positive thing—even among Christians. Several years ago, I (Doug) was conducting a singles' workshop on sexuality. As I shared the topic with a Christian leader friend, his immediate response was, "Two hours on single sexuality? How many ways can you say *don't*?" I sadly reflected on this response, realizing that simplistic "don'ts" around sexual behaviors will never create sincere joy, healthy intimacy, or godly discipline.

Like it or not, God in his infinite wisdom didn't create you with a switch inside your brain that could be turned on the first night of your honeymoon. *Your sexuality, with both your gender and your desires, permeates everything about your life and relationships.* It creates the full range of human emotions, including love, confusion, pleasure, despair, curiosity, and disappointment. Your sexuality has been responsible for both genuine intimate bonding and regretfully immature experiences—perhaps even traumatic ones you'd just as soon forget.

We All Have a Story

The range of experiences and attitudes among single adults with respect to their sexuality is so varied and complex—producing both fulfillment *and* frustration. Consider just a few examples:

13

Since high school, Jenny typically has become sexually involved with guys she "loves." Jack is coming off a divorce and is thankful to be in a healthier relationship than his failed marriage. They both attend a great church and have recently become convicted about their sexual involvement together. However, neither can understand why God would want only married people to have sex. Why not a couple committed to each other and seriously considering marriage?

Ashley becomes tearful each time she thinks back to that special dinner with her dad: "Sweetheart, you know how proud I am of you and the beautiful woman you've become. I want you to promise me you'll patiently wait for marriage before fully giving yourself sexually to a man." Then he reached across the table and placed the wonderful promise ring on her finger. How that moment has sustained her resolve through some very romantic relationships! She is so glad she was encouraged to consider her values and keep her commitment to purity.

John shrank deep into his chair when his men's group leader asked what the group thought about masturbation. He could readily identify with the guilt some members confessed had plagued them surrounding the behavior. John appreciated the chance to start creating a practical theology for masturbation and thinking through how to handle his fantasy life. "No wonder I don't feel right masturbating to fantasies about Misty. She's my sister's best friend, for goodness' sake—but man, is she sexy!"

Pam experienced sexual abuse as a child and later had an abortion. Healthy boundaries have never really been a part of her life. Consequently, she now avoids anything romantic. She has recoiled into an isolative shell intended to protect her from pain and her choices—but mostly to protect her from herself. The extra weight she carries serves as a protective firewall, announcing to potential suitors that she no longer has a desire to be a sexual being. They would do well to look elsewhere.

Ted finds girls sexually aggressive and feels insecure around them. He hopes Gina is different. But in typical fashion, his insecurities prevent him from taking the risk of making more than her acquaintance. So he longingly observes her from a distance. Rather than going outside his comfort zone to develop healthy social skills with women, Ted instead reaches out to the allure of Internet porn—women who never reject him and always greet him with an inviting smile. He feels more confident about himself in this world of pseudo-relationships. It does ease his loneliness . . . for a while. However, he ultimately feels even more isolated and inadequate when he reenters the real world of trying to relate with women.

These represent but a few examples of the sexual journeys of thousands of single adults just like you—so diverse, so full of joy, so full of confusion. Precious brother or sister, we wish we knew *your* story. Our struggles and our victories have much in common—having often been shaped more by our hearts and attitudes than by our behaviors. We have prayed for you while writing this book—that it would guide, heal, and enrich your sexual journey in a deeply personal and practical way.

Why We Wrote This Book

Our heart's desire is to help Christian single adults sort through and find better answers about their sexuality—to not just repress or tolerate their sexuality but to redefine and celebrate it! Each of the authors comes from our own background of experiences in dealing with single sexuality.

I (Doug) grew up in a conservative missionary home and stayed single until age twenty-seven, quite repressed and dating very little. I was divorced at thirty-seven before marrying my lovely wife, Catherine. I can easily identify with those who find themselves in a place they never imagined—desperately single or single again. I've also watched my daughter, Merrill, go through her own journey as a twentysomething single adult. At times so much peer influence seemed to weigh on her that she appeared almost helpless to counteract the culture.

I (Michael Todd), on the other hand, am a late-thirties, never-married, single adult who is "waiting for his Eve." I'm a part of an increasingly large group of single adults waiting until later in life to marry. As one desiring to remain faithful until my wedding day, I'd be lying if I didn't confess that some days I find waiting extremely difficult. And though I am still a physical virgin (by the grace of God), my soul virginity has been compromised more times than I care to recall. But on my most difficult days, I now find it helpful to remind myself that how I live out my sexuality is intended to be a reflection of God and *his* character. My life is tied to a much larger story.

That's part of what this book is about: giving single adults a wide-angle lens through which to see the bigger picture of their sexuality. We desire to help you create a theology that goes beyond mere "do's and don'ts," providing practical explanations of why and how to wait within the Creator's awesome plan. We want to take you on a journey of growth and healing as you learn to experience your true sexual identity in the context of wonderfully intimate relationships that are both healthy and godly.

A Glimpse into the Journey of a Soul Virgin

Before we travel too far, we want to give you a brief working definition for *soul virgin*:

> *A soul virgin is one who continuously seeks to value, celebrate, and protect God's design for sexuality—body, soul, and spirit—in oneself and others.*

We want to help single adults establish practical models for God's design regarding sexuality. That design should be evident in all aspects of our lives—body, soul, and spirit. A soul virgin has a desire not only to consider God's viewpoint about the importance of our sexuality (value) but also to enjoy it (celebrate) and to do what's necessary to guard its worth (protect) in his or her life and in the lives of others. And although soul virginity begins in single adulthood, the concept continues to apply into married, single-again, or widowed life as well. *This makes the pledge of soul virginity a lifetime commitment.*

Because our sexuality is ultimately more about relational intimacy than just the physical act of sex, we've decided to break up our journey into three major sections, with the conclusion reserved as a bit of parting encouragement. You'll find many new terms and concepts along the path as we introduce a whole new language, offering fresh perspective to weary travelers.

Chapters 1 through 6 will highlight our need for *intimacy with God*—by far our most important need. Without clarity in this relationship, you can't really hope to have healthy and fulfilling relationships with others or with a potential mate.

[handwritten margin note: begins in adolescence]

16

We'll discuss how God uses our sexuality to draw us into intimacy with himself (chapter 1) and create helpful new terms and models to more effectively understand sexuality (chapter 2). We'll develop how to prioritize heart-directed behaviors rather than ones determined by the two extremes of legalism and raw erotic feelings (chapter 3) and explore the importance of a lifelong commitment to becoming a soul virgin (chapter 4), along with God's provision for dealing with our failures and shortcomings (chapter 5) and how to recognize and enjoy contentment as a single person (chapter 6).

Chapters 7 through 11 will highlight our need for intimacy with God's people. We'll talk about masculinity (chapter 7), femininity (chapter 8), what to do with erotic sexual desires (chapter 9), how to honor others sexually (chapter 10), and the importance of relating with the opposite sex in non-romantic, non-erotic relationships (chapter 11).

Chapters 12 through 15 will discuss what intimacy with God's possible soul mate looks like when we pursue a marriage partner God's way. We'll use the term Coupling for romantic relationships and walk together through the three stages of Coupling: considering, confirming, and committing (chapter 12). We'll expose seven viruses that destroy romantic relationships (chapter 13), discuss why both law and grace are needed when defining coupling relationships (chapter 14), and share the importance of romantic relationships that grow slowly with intention and are properly balanced (chapter 15). Finally, chapter 16 will promote the benefits of being single adults who are sexually alive—in ways often taken for granted.

You will see the pronoun "we" used throughout the text. Both of us (Doug and Michael Todd) attempt to speak with one voice where possible. When you read one of us speaking in the first person, you should assume it's Doug—after all, Doug was already writing about sexuality when Michael Todd was still in diapers! When someone else is speaking, their name (Michael Todd, Vickie, etc.) will be used in parentheses to distinguish their voices from Doug's. Where Scripture is referenced directly or indirectly, we will note its location in parentheses and commend it to you for further study.

Placing God at the Center

From the outset, we should let you in on an important secret. This process of becoming a soul virgin is not one you can undertake in your own strength. You'll need to rely on the power of God in your life for this. Each of us, regardless of our sexual histories, has compromised his or her soul virginity to some extent in this fallen and sin-diseased world. While physical virginity is something you can *lose*, soul virginity is something you can *grow by becoming*. But without God at the center of your life, none of this will even make sense. Unless you recognize God's claim on your life—especially your sexual life—you will find no compelling reason to buy into or even consider the concepts of this book.

However, if you recognize your place in the universe as God's creation and the importance of his guidance in your life, you'll be able to see this book as a sort of "hitchhiker's guide" along the twists and turns of your sexual journey. And unlike the Hollywood movie, we believe there *is* a Creator God responsible for our existence who knows best how we were designed to function. Understanding this, it only makes sense to follow his "blueprint" for our lives—especially when it comes to the area of sexuality.

Soul virginity, then, becomes a lifestyle *regardless* of the presence or absence of your own physical virginity. The loving Creator joins each of us in the place we find ourselves sexually, enabling us to value, celebrate, and protect his gift of sexuality as we move forward and seek to understand his overall purpose for it.

We hope by now you have a taste for the passion behind why we've chosen to write on this topic. Our desire is for soul virgins to start a revolution among Christian single adults— singles who believe "true love waits" but find themselves needing more than "just don't" in order to pursue sexual purity and wholeness. *We desperately need a larger purpose for our sexuality, enabling us to rise above our own selfish struggles and to find life-changing meaning.* But to catch God's vision for the larger story, we must first go back to the place where it all began.

Part 1:

Intimacy with God

One

God's Design in Sexuality

A Celebration of Intimacy

Principle:
We are created as intimate sexual beings

The almighty Trinity was on a creative roll, having fun planning out their human being love adventure. They'd decided to create a world and populate it with humans but were discussing how to help these finite creatures understand the infinite Jehovah. Ultimately, they would accomplish this through the living parable of Jesus—"God with us." But they also wanted to create illustrations and experiences that would reveal God's character and his relationship with them.

Nature (the created heavens and earth) was a marvelous part of that revelation. How the Trinity must have enjoyed creating each metaphor. God could be illustrated as a solid rock, Jesus as a living stream, and the Holy Spirit as a gentle and powerful wind. Mountains would reveal the strength of God's creative power, and sunsets would evoke an appreciation for his artistic beauty.

The Creator also wanted to demonstrate his essence of love to his creation. After all, God had been enjoying perfect fellowship with himself in eternity past through the Holy Trinity. He desired his creation to understand that they could find true happiness and completeness only through intimate relationships—first with God, then with others. At this point, divine creativity and imagination reached its peak: "Then God said, 'Let us make man in our image' . . . *Male and female he created them*" (Genesis 1:26–27, emphasis added). Scholars tell us these verses are poetic in style and use a form of parallelism that actually equates the "image of God" with "male and female." God created our *sexuality* to display his very image, suggesting that both masculinity and femininity are required to fully mirror the divine character.

God's Grand Demonstration

God is a deeply relational being who created humankind to experience and reflect his own image of love and creativity. Sexuality became his grand demonstration of intimacy. He chose to do this by creating amazingly different but complexly interactive genders (male and female) with two important types of sexual relating: gender and erotic.

God gave us a glimpse into his very nature with our masculinity and femininity and the magnetic way they attract, complement, and relate with one another. Creating *gender* produced such concepts as father and mother, brother and sister, initiating and responding, strength and nurturing. God created Adam and Eve to begin the first family and to be the father and mother of us all.

He also made Adam and Eve the first lovers, each with *erotic* longing to complete the other. Can you imagine the excitement and awe Adam felt the first time he gazed upon his Eve and she alluringly touched his very soul? They deeply desired each other spiritually, emotionally, mentally, socially, and physically. But that's not all. Their "naked and unashamed" sexual relationship set the stage for a beautiful illustration that would tell the most remarkable story of all. God artistically formed the marital relationship to display the personal love relationship God desires spiritually with each one of us.

Perfect Intimacy: Reflected and Retold

In some sense, this divine story is retold every time someone falls in love. In its purest form, a young man seeks a bride, passionately looking for her. When he finds her, she is awakened by his love and desires to embrace his strength. He is enthralled with her innate beauty and receptive longing for him. They've never quite known what they were missing before this moment, but now they must have what the other so tenderly possesses.

He invites her into a relationship, and their journey begins. They pledge their lives to one another and look forward to the elaborate wedding that awaits them. It will be a time when two wonderfully matched hearts and bodies will finally unite under the blessing of their friends, their family, and their God. Those in attendance will hold the couple accountable to fulfill the vows they've made to each other—"for better or for worse." When the ceremony is complete, the couple seals their wedding vows by sharing together something that is meant for the other—their true sex. *They will share this special relationship with no one else for the rest of their lives.* Their one-flesh sexual intimacy becomes the seal of their love, distinguishing their relationship from all others and echoing the beautiful imagery found in Song of Songs 8:6: "Place me like a seal over your heart, like a seal on your arm; for love . . . burns like blazing fire, like a mighty flame."

This story is a reflection of Christ's love for his bride, the Church. He seeks her out and finds her, awakening her to something she's never known before and inviting her to journey with him. Desperately desiring him, she eagerly follows. This is where we currently find ourselves in this marvelous story of redemption: pledged to Christ and awaiting his return, when he will take his bride to the grand wedding feast to be with him forever.

Telling the Story through Broken Reflectors

Doesn't the beauty of that story take your breath away and stir something deep within your soul? This metaphor is rarely taught to Christian singles. As immature and sinful people, so much interferes with our ability to play out romantic relationships as God intended. Quite often, our actual experience comes off as a rather poor reflection of the ideal. Nonetheless, this ideal *is* the Creator's intention for our sexuality—the goal to which we should aspire.

Actually, this provides a good backdrop for our journey into single adult sexuality. We so easily wander off track and forget that sexuality was intended to be a window into the very heart of the Trinity—created to reveal the great value God places on intimate connecting. His sexual verbs are "relate," "love," and "connect"—not "score," "get some," or "get it on."

The Road Map to Sexual Wholeness

These are not easy times to be struggling as single adults with issues of sexuality. We face many challenges living in a culture that is blatantly hostile to Christian values. The average age of marriage is advancing toward thirty, and casual premarital sex is widely accepted—even in many churches.

In thinking about redefining single sexuality, we ran across a humorous story about a young lady who'd been driving around for some time with a growing sense of irritation. Upset that her every effort led nowhere, she finally concluded she was truly lost. At the onset of a migraine, she stopped for directions.

"Where am I?" the young lady asked in frustration.

"You're in Greenville," replied the gas station attendant in a kindly tone.

"How do I go from Greenville to Union City?" she bluntly inquired.

The attendant pondered her exasperated question and then reluctantly replied, "I wouldn't try to get there from here."

So it is with trying to get to sexual wholeness from the backdrop of MTV, reality dating shows, and so many other pop-culture influences. In the chasm between a distorted but vocal Hollywood and a sometimes piously silent church, single adults frequently aren't sure where to turn for directions. Deep down, they know they're lost but aren't quite sure what direction to take on the road map of life to reach a godly destination. How interesting that so many singles begin their journey into sexual wholeness hoping for only slight changes in direction, but end up realizing they need a whole new paradigm—a whole new way of thinking.

A new paradigm is ultimately what this book is about. It's about discarding ineffective thinking and unhealthy behaviors, creating new attitudes and helpful answers. It's also about beginning to ask the right questions. Not "How do I go from Greenville to Union City?" but rather "How do I tear down and *reconstruct* Greenville so that it *becomes* Union City?"

Here's an example of what we mean by immature "Greenville" thinking. We've all heard singles ask the proverbial question "How far can I go?" when it comes to premarital physical intimacy. By itself, this is the wrong question. It treats erotic sexual interactions as a selfish behavior, pushing the boundary's outer limits to manipulate the greatest sexual buzz possible. Here are some more mature questions in light of God's design for sexuality: "In our romantic interactions, how can we find sexual wholeness and healthy intimacy in ways *pleasing to God*?" "How can I *steward* my partner's sexuality and develop his or her true potential to become all God wants him or her to be?" "How can I value, celebrate, and protect this other person, who might be *someone else's* Adam or Eve?" If we want to get to Union City, Greenville thinking won't get us there.

Someone has wisely stated that the resources, attitudes, and philosophies that have created a problem will always be inadequate to solve the problem. We challenge you: *ask God to help you bring something new and profound to this issue of single-adult sexuality—something very different from the echoes of* Seinfeld *and* Friends *from one side of the chasm and the cries of "just don't" and rigid prohibitions from the other.* We need something to have an impact on our very souls—something that will revolutionize our behaviors *and* our hearts.

Two

God's Sexual Economy

Practical Skills and Models

Principle:
Healthy sexual intimacy requires many deliberate choices

Much of our confusion in single adult sexuality comes from poorly defined concepts and inadequate road maps for the sexual journey toward loving connection. How frustrating that we so often struggle with having an adequate vocabulary to describe sexual intimacy. Words become loaded with baggage or are too vague or adolescent. For example, the concepts "sex," "dating," and "virgin" have such varied meaning unless they're carefully defined. In our morally relativistic culture, each person seems to define terms according to their own background or to their own personal advantage, with no truth to guide their hearts and actions. As authors, we have been challenged to create new terms and models as we've struggled to understand what these ideas really mean within the Creator's purposeful design.

We will refer to God's viewpoint regarding sexuality as *God's sexual economy*. During biblical times, a person working as a steward or manager of a given area of household responsibility would carefully manage according to an *economy*, or a wise set of principles or household rules. Similarly, the Creator has established sexuality within an "economy"—principles and guidelines—to lead us into the very heart of the matter: the enjoyment of intimate relationships.

Honest Dialogue and Deliberate Choices

Before introducing our models, let's discuss briefly two crucial skills for utilizing them successfully. Single adults are often confused about sexuality because they seldom communicate openly about this part of their relationships. Assumptions, hidden agendas, and confusion abound. Mature singles have grown to a place of *honest dialogue*, able to comfortably bring up and discuss sexual and romantic topics with questions such as "Since we both struggle sexually, how are we going to deal with it?" or "I've really enjoyed getting to know you better these past couple of months. I would like to become a couple. What do you think?"

We must practice honesty for any genuine intimacy to occur: "Therefore, each of you must put off falsehood and speak truthfully" (Ephesians 4:25). Only through open dialogue and "speaking the truth in love" (v. 15) will singles create the intimate and fulfilling sexual relating each desires.

Single adults can also create a mess with friendships and premarital relationships by not making *deliberate choices*. We get this complaint so often, especially concerning single men: "He won't decide where we are in the relationship, so we just putz along." Part of our being in God's image is that we have a "will" for making intentional decisions. We aren't ruled by raw emotions or chemistry. We can decide when and how we want to be sexual—or not be. Think of Scripture's wise advice: "I want you to promise, O women of Jerusalem, not to awaken love until the time is right" (Song of Songs 8:4 NLT). So many erotic sexual behaviors occur due to inadequate planning and spur-of-the-moment impulsiveness rather than intentional decision-making. As you consider the following models, remember: *honest dialogue and wise, deliberate choices will both create and guard appropriately intimate relationships.*

The Boxes of Sexuality: Defining Our Terms

Do you remember Jenny and Jack from the introduction? They were Christians desiring God's best but couldn't understand why God would want only married people to enjoy sex. The following pair of models certainly would have helped their confusion. Throughout our journey together, we'll be referring to these three concepts: *sexuality, erotic sexual*

28

behavior, and *true sex* (the act of sexual intercourse and, as far as we are concerned, other things that might as well be). These *Boxes of Sexuality* can be distinguished from one another like this:

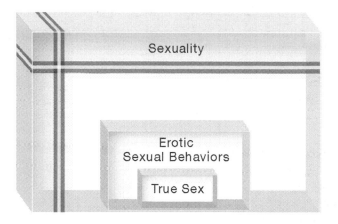

Perhaps a true story from early in one of our colleagues' marriage might serve as a helpful illustration. With a big grin on his face, Vickie's husband Wayne brought her a large box one year for her birthday. She opened the package to find an assortment of jazz CDs, which were some of her favorites. Vickie and Wayne had been friends for a few years before becoming a couple. Music was something he'd always known was important to her. Inside the large box was also a medium-sized box. Upon opening it, she found a number of striking, personally selected gifts for the home he knew she wanted. During their time as a premarital couple, Wayne came to appreciate her taste in decor. His gifts showed thoughtful attentiveness and that he cherished what was important to her.

Then to her surprise Vickie found a tiny box hidden deep within the second box. When she unwrapped this smallest box, she was thrilled to discover a blue topaz ring, more special and costly by far than any of the other gifts. The brilliant color of the topaz reminded her of their honeymoon and the beautiful blue sea of the Mediterranean.

This story superbly illustrates our Boxes of Sexuality. Take another look at our model and imagine them as the gift boxes Vickie received for her birthday. The largest box contained gifts that reminded her of her early friendship with Wayne. *Sexuality* (as we'll define it in this book) is something we experience relationally with all people, including friends and family. *Sexuality is the large box all of us live in.* It contains our general sexual desire and gender makeup (masculine and feminine) that propel each of us to seek out intimate connection—with another person, with a spouse, or with God.

This broad sexual identity includes a variety of elements such as our maleness and femaleness with our soft and strong traits, our desires with urges and attractions, our social interactivity with flirtatiousness and playfulness, and the set of values that direct our relational interactions. We are intentionally using the term *sexuality* because the word *sex* is often taken to mean intercourse. Sexuality is much broader and more all-inclusive.

Sexuality is really more of a soul thing. Our bodies might give us visual input and hormonal arousal, but we interpret and build on these sexual cues using our minds, hearts, and wills. Unlike those in the animal kingdom, humans *make choices* to create erotic arousal. We can pursue sexual feelings or not. Our sexuality is often only 20 percent body-driven and 80 percent mind-driven. God gave us the ability to create mental imagery and fantasies through what we see and feel. These imaginings enhance our enjoyment of the opposite sex, though this also must be disciplined to prevent sinful lusting: "So think clearly and exercise self-control. . . . Don't slip back into your old ways of doing evil; you didn't know any better then" (1 Peter 1:13–14 NLT).

An important part of sexuality involves how we handle our sexual desires and attractions. Let's face it: men and women get turned on. Some of this is hormonal; however, the bigger picture of God's design for our hormones is to push us toward relational intimacy, not just erotically "hooking up" or creating the release of tension through masturbation.

You'll notice this largest box of sexuality is much bigger than the other two boxes. This is because it also includes items that are about relational intimacy of the soul. Sexuality describes *who we are* more than what we do. You are at your very core a sexual being, whether or not you ever engage in any sexual behaviors. It isn't possible for humans to do anything relationally—talk on the phone with a friend, play a board game, or even type this chapter for you to read—without expressing some aspect of our sexuality.

The second of Vickie's gift boxes was found inside the largest box and contained personal gifts unique to her, presents that could be given only by someone who knew her more intimately. Likewise, within the large box of sexuality are two smaller gift-wrapped boxes—gifts some singles may never choose to give or receive. This second box will be opened and enjoyed only by those who deliberately choose to enter into a coupling relationship. This box includes a variety of *erotic sexual behaviors*—activities considered romantic or arousing. Erotic sexual behaviors include mental actions (such as erotic fantasy, love letters, and sex talk) as well as physical actions (such as kissing and caressing).

Inside the erotic sexual behaviors box is the smallest gift box of *true sex*. Like the precious ring Vickie received in her tiny gift box, "true sex" involves the most intimate of erotic sexual behaviors. This special little box was intended by God to remain unopened until that most intimate of relationships—marriage.

In God's sexual economy, true sex is *at minimum* defined as sexual intercourse (see Hebrews 13:4). Whether oral sex, anal sex, and mutual orgasms should be included here is often questioned (at least by our culture), thanks to Hollywood and political figures who debate whether oral sex is really sex after all. For the thinking Christian, however, we strongly suggest that the only appropriate place for these behaviors (along with their related orgasms) is in the category of "true sex." We are in no way necessarily endorsing all these behaviors for every married couple. We are simply stating that we believe *all intercourse behavior (oral, anal, vaginal) and mutual orgasms are biblically inappropriate outside of a committed marital union.*

Remember, true sex was given as a picture of the complete intimacy between Christ and his Bride, the Church. As such, all expressions of erotic sexuality should honor and derive their meaning from marital lovemaking. The gift box of erotic sexual behaviors in premarital relationships will always be incomplete, pointing toward true sex in marriage. And although true sex in marriage completes the earthly metaphor, it too remains an incomplete and "dimly reflected" mirror of the *ultimate* intimacy our souls truly long for—a deep need for intimacy that will be fully satisfied only by *God himself* at the end of the divine love story in heaven (Revelation 21:1–7).

31

The Relationship Continuum Bridge

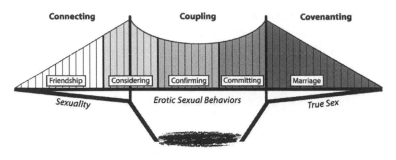

The Relationship Continuum Bridge: Defining Intimate Sexual Relationships

A *continuum* can be understood as a path along which things progress in logical fashion. To better understand God's design, the *Relationship Continuum Bridge* will help us navigate our way through intimate relationships in a meaningful sequence. Three distinct relationships develop along a road that leads to the covenant of marriage and true sex. This first and third relationship on the continuum (Connecting and Covenanting) are valid in their own right. One isn't godlier than the other; God uses each to accomplish his purposes throughout our lives. The middle relationship (Coupling) is best understood as a "bridge" between the other two. Only one coupling relationship will eventually progress onward to Covenanting. All others will eventually return back to Connecting. With this basic understanding, let's take a look at each one separately.

Connecting Relationships

Connecting relationships contain many familiar ideas, including both friendships and the behavior of "casual" dating. The term "Connecting" helps us understand that sexual connecting actually begins from our earliest gender interactions with our moms and dads. This part of the continuum in singleness includes sexual desire and erotic surges; however, the emphasis of connecting relationships is on friendships and opposite-sex interactions for growth and enjoyment in groups and pairs. The focus is on skill-building in relationships with the opposite sex—*not* erotic sexual behaviors.

Single adults will have any number of connecting relationships at a given time, regardless of whether they are actively seeking a mate or not. Eventually, a possible soul mate may appear who prompts them to pursue group dates or even more deliberate one-on-one time together to get acquainted more intimately. Consideration about exclusive dating may take place in Connecting, but no decision about exclusivity has yet been made. Men and women can enjoy these attractions in Connecting while intentionally maintaining healthy boundaries, guarding their hearts, and engaging in honest dialogue.

Notice from the Relationship Continuum Bridge that the experience of each other's sexuality (the largest of the sexuality boxes) can be considerably enjoyed even in Connecting. *However, erotic sexual behaviors and true sex are considered inappropriate, unhealthy, and outside of God's design for connecting relationships.*

Coupling Relationships

Coupling involves three unique decision-making stages: *considering, confirming,* and *committing.* Many couples stay in confusion because they never make deliberate choices or know exactly "where the relationship is." What initiates a coupling relationship is a decision to become exclusive. In reference to the animal kingdom, sometimes the word *coupling* becomes synonymous with the idea of *mating.* We aren't using this word in quite that sense. Instead, we emphasize that Coupling does begin the mating *process.*

The process begins with the *considering* stage, which actually most often begins in connecting relationships. From the first date to the time two people deliberately define their relationship as exclusive, the considering stage takes place in Connecting. Erotic sexual behaviors have no place in this "getting to know you" time, as it will only serve to confuse the discovery process of the other person for who they really are. Consideration of the other person's suitability as a life partner is also likely taking place in Connecting.

However, at a point in time, an honest discussion leads to a deliberate choice to become an exclusive couple (Coupling). As a new "item," the couple begins exploring whether marriage potential exists. Physical romance in the form of erotic sexual behaviors becomes a comfortable part of expressing love—to an extent. Each couple will need to negotiate which behaviors they will and will not allow into their relationship, all the while recognizing true sex as being biblically reserved for the covenanting relationship of marriage (chapters 12 through 15 are dedicated to helping couples work through these questions from a biblical framework).

Confirming is the stage when a couple is "engaged to be engaged." From our experience counseling young couples, this seems to be the most neglected element of premarital relationships. As the decision to marry settles on a couple, we firmly believe couples at this stage should seek premarital counseling and have open discussions about their future together. Topics such as children, STDs, sexual pasts, financial budgeting, gender role expectations, religious preferences, family skeletons, and other intimate issues should be shared in a trusting environment. This is the time to put all the cards on the table, before commitments are made and wedding invitations are sent—*before* the pressure is too great to allow them to back out of a less-than-ideal marriage. For couples who stay the course toward marriage, those practicing this stage of Coupling will find a greater freedom to delay engagement and wedding plans for a short time (if necessary) to more adequately address issues that arise from confirming. We believe they will also greatly reduce their risk of divorce in the early years of marriage resulting from unrealistic expectations about their mates.

Committing is the engagement stage of Coupling. It includes a formal proposal of marriage, though it may or may not involve an engagement ring. Specific plans evolve with wedding logistics and the practical preparation of joining two lives forever. If the couple has successfully navigated the confirming stage, they will likely find this stage less emotionally tense than those who didn't. The formal engagement can potentially be relatively short, taking only as long as the practical elements of mailing invitations and planning the wedding and honeymoon.

Covenanting Relationships

Covenanting cements the one-flesh companionship of marriage. With the final "I do's," the relationship is forever changed. In God's eyes, soul mates have formed and complete lovemaking (true sex) is shared *within the safety of a lifelong commitment to one another.* The high level of trust created by such a commitment or covenant bond becomes God's vehicle for true erotic fulfillment. From the viewpoint of God's ideal, perhaps it's now easier to see why all premarital erotic expression to this point have at best been incomplete.

Though many in our society view marriage as a needless formality, God views marriage as a covenant between two lives that are forever bonded. All prior connecting and coupling relationships have served as preparation for this remarkable love relationship now consummated—a beautiful metaphor for Christ and his bride.

3-D Sexuality: The Interwoven Facets of Body, Soul, and Spirit

In developing his metaphor of sexual intimacy, the Almighty gave men and women three dimensions to their gender sexuality and sexual desire: body, soul, and spirit. Recognizing the importance of this concept, the apostle Paul prayed, "Now may God himself, the God of peace, make you pure. . . . May your whole self—spirit, soul, and body—be kept safe and without fault" (1 Thessalonians 5:23 NCV). Perhaps Paul even named spirit and soul first due to their greater importance.

These three facets of the self are interwoven dimensions rather than separate parts. They interact together to create the expressions of sexuality within intimate relationships. Our *body* wonderfully combines hormones, blood vessels, nerves, and skin to create attraction and desire. Our *soul* involves our mind and imagination, our will and our choice, our heart and our emotions. Our *spirit* gives us true love and creates an ability to become "one flesh" with another (Genesis 2:24). Understanding our 3-D sexuality is crucial for single adults to experience deeper friendships and fulfilling romantic relationships.

As you expand your understanding of the many facets of body, soul, and spirit, deeper and more meaningful intimacy will occur. Think through each of the following aspects of sexuality, considering how you as a single adult might enjoy them in your own connecting and coupling relationships.

Body: Subtle body distinctions such as hands, mouth, and ear lobes; nonverbal body expressions of feeling, such as excitement and fatigue; verbal nuances such as pitch, tone, and rate; nurturing and protective gestures (opening doors, offering assistance in need, etc.).

> Examples: "Your accent is incredibly sexy." "Your dimples make me smile."

Soul: Varied emotional responses to situations; listening with understanding; enjoying gender differences; engaging interactively in creative forms of play; dreaming, conversing, and imagining together; enjoying deeper connection with others by lowering defensive walls.

> Examples: "I love the way you laugh." "I enjoyed our discussion about world events."

Spirit: Reflecting God's love more fully; finding completion in intimate relationships; actively encouraging others in their personal walk with God; intuitive thought; listening deeply for the Holy Spirit's leading.

> Example: "Your excitement about the mission trip to Costa Rica stirs my heart for God, too." "Your freedom in worship is so attractive to me."

We frequently draw too great a distinction between single and married adults. The sexual skills and disciplines learned in the crucible of singleness apply for a lifetime. For example, Sally appreciates her husband Jim's ability to enjoy other women as whole people rather than seeing them merely as body parts or sex objects. During their Coupling, Jim explained to her that this was a more recently acquired skill. He'd been challenged at a seminar to treat women as three-dimensional people. Now when he noticed a sexy woman at the mall, he gave her a soul and a life as he noticed in her face that she was tired. He looked at the packages she was carrying and wondered what her life was like and who the packages were for. He thought about her desire to love and respect her husband, knowing fully it wasn't him. He also prayed for her, that she would come to know Christ if she didn't already. This helped

Sally realize that his lovemaking with her truly reflected his ability to see her own soul-sexiness and to connect deeply beyond just her body.

Putting It All Together

The concepts and definitions presented in this chapter aren't the only way to understand God's intent for sexuality and romantic relationships. We simply present them as models that we hope will help you understand God's greater purpose behind your sexuality as a single adult. But as you'll come to see throughout our journey, disciplining your behaviors is only half the story. It's also a matter of the heart.

Three
Living Boldly from Your Heart

Principle:
Godly attitudes should determine sexual behaviors

Wouldn't it be helpful if guilt and fear always motivated godly change and "scared us straight"? Most of us can empathize with the poor bird a young lady once bought for companionship. To her dismay, not only did the parrot know how to speak, but his language was much too colorful. One day in utter frustration she threatened, "One more dirty word and I'm putting you in the freezer!" Sure enough, he used one of his choice words, and into the freezer he went. Within twenty seconds he was pecking and scratching to be let out. He squawked, "I'll never say another dirty word again!" The woman had pity on the bird and let him out. After three months with no more bad language, she asked him, "What changed your attitude?" to which the bird replied, "What in the world did that chicken do?"

While threats may work for a while, external constraints won't motivate your sexual behaviors over the long haul. Your heart attitudes—*your internal motivations*—are what really count.

God and Our Hearts

While God has always cared about our behaviors, he cares much more about our heart and attitudes. When Scripture refers to the *heart*, it's not talking about being driven by your feelings and raw emotion. That's a more romantic view of the heart, one that permeates our culture. Instead, the heart refers to the core of who you are, the deepest and truest part of your soul—your attitudes, motives, and mind-set (see Matthew 15:17–20).

Does this mean your sexual behaviors aren't important as long as your heart is right? Of course not. Scripture says they go hand in hand. God cares about right actions *and* right motives—clean hands and a pure heart (see Psalm 24:3–4). But here's the good news: *A heart surrendered to God produces godly behaviors that are directed by God's heart.* If the attitude of your heart is truly to please God, surrendering ownership of yourself and your sexuality to his plan for your life, God's desires will become your desires (Psalm 37:4). *Your hearts will become synchronized.*

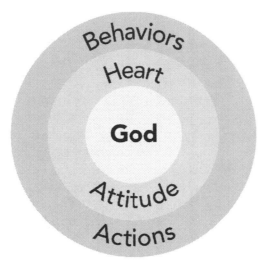

Two Ungodly Extremes: Legalistic Repression and Christian Hedonism

The above diagram will help illustrate how single adults can better discipline and enjoy their sexuality. Historically, the Church has overemphasized behaviors when telling singles how to handle their sexuality. Dwelling in this outer circle of behaviors tends to produce one of two extreme results.

The first is *legalistic repression.* I grew up with a legalistic list of "do's and don'ts" that primarily consisted of "don'ts." It was sort of like this: "don't, don't, don't, don't, don't, *do*, don't, don't. . . ." And what was the one "do"? Something like kissing before marriage—but only with a chaperone present.

For me, the "don'ts" were all externally imposed by the Church and the "sex police" (my parents, chaperones, pastors, etc.). These "don'ts" weren't very effective in high school and college, especially as I gained more and more independence. Advice such as "true love waits" is good; but without practical explanation of *how* and *why* it waits, such encouragement can only last so long. It eventually breaks down without something deeper and more substantial driving it. This ineffective focus on outlawing behaviors frequently results in repression rather than godly discipline. Legalistic singles ban *behaviors*, hoping this will protect their *hearts* and drive them closer to *God*. This is approaching godliness from the *outside in* and looks something like the diagram on the next page.

Single adults with this approach to godliness are often surprised when their sexual surges overwhelm their genuine desire to make godly choices in their behavior. Unfortunately, they've never learned to make godly choices motivated from God's heart. They've simply repressed their sexual feelings and behaviors rather than accepting and disciplining them.

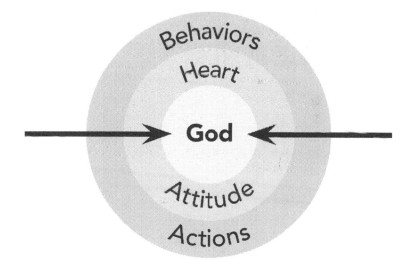

Think of repression as trying to choke your sexual desires into submission. Ultimately, you'll grow tired and give in. This method is destined for failure. On the other hand, *godly discipline* understands that sexual desires are more than hormonal. The person acting from discipline learns skills for *directing* their yearnings in godly ways without having to choke and fight them all the time.

The second result of trying to live in the outer circle (with behavioral rules only) swings to the opposite extreme. We call this *Christian hedonism*, a lifestyle of indulgence in which everything but vaginal intercourse is considered acceptable behavior for premarital couples. A single woman once stated in counseling that she was technically a virgin because no one had ever ejaculated in her vagina. [How sad that some Christian singles working the behavior circle try to avoid "sex" because they want to remain "technical virgins"—but have no idea what virginity is really all about.]

A significant problem exists when Christians legalistically and behaviorally define sex as merely vaginal intercourse. As long as a penis has never been in a vagina, they consider themselves virgins. By ignoring the thoughts and attitudes of their hearts, those who follow this approach leave open all other forms of sexual behavior—including oral and anal sex—since these don't violate their strict legalistic code.

In a study of 20,000 adolescents between 1997 and 2002, the federally funded National Longitudinal Study of Adolescent Health found a statistically significant increase in "high-risk behaviors" between those who took seriously their abstinence pledges (13 percent) and those who made no such pledge (2 percent).[1] What this seems to imply is that even Christian teens who pledge abstinence more often either (a) break their pledge "accidentally" by having unprotected vaginal intercourse or, more likely, (b) intentionally engage in unprotected oral and anal intercourse as "alternatives" to vaginal intercourse. Of course, they don't call it oral sex or anal sex because it "isn't really sex" by their definition. Instead, oral intercourse might conveniently be called "giving head" or "getting a blow job."

This completely misses God's heart. So many Christian singles develop their romantic relationships with total nudity, orgasms, or mutual masturbation but with little regard to the deeper issues of morality other than that they're "not having sex." Jesus chided the religious rulers of his day for being so focused on external behaviors that they missed the more important matters of the heart: "Woe to you, teachers of the law and Pharisees, you hypocrites! You clean the outside of the cup and dish, but inside they are full of greed and self-indulgence. . . . *First clean the inside of the cup and dish, and then the outside also will be clean"* (Matthew 23:25–26, emphasis added).

Living from the Inside Out

Working from the outside in—that is, regulating behaviors to produce godlier attitudes that hopefully lead us closer to God—produces rather poor results. Instead, God wants us to live from the *inside out*. Seeking God's heart first will allow your own heart to be transformed by the Holy Spirit, which will over time produce more purity in your behavior. Let's take a closer look at the three aspects of this process: God, heart, and behavior.

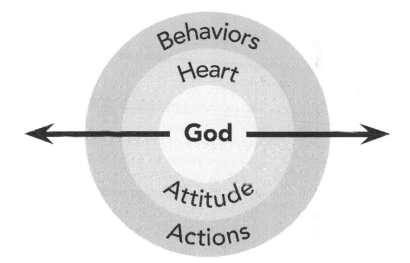

First, as with everything in the Christian experience, the process must start with your own personal relationship with *God*. Commit to understanding God's heart and what he says is best for you. What does God say directly and indirectly through the principles found in Scripture? What character traits and heart attitudes does he desire? Why do those traits and attitudes reflect God's sexual economy? You may never fully understand God's reasoning for all he asks of you, but pursuing God as a matter of *first priority* will help you develop a trust relationship with him—a trust to anchor you as you move toward the outer circles of heart and behavior.

Second, an intimate relationship with God will over time transform your *heart*. God wants to shape your heart and your attitudes using the principles in Scripture that flow from *his* heart. The process of conforming your heart to God's will leads to deep spiritual maturity over time: "Don't become so well-adjusted to your culture that you fit into it without even thinking. Instead, fix your attention on God. You'll be changed from the inside out" (Romans 12:2 Message). *If you ask God for his will and seek his heart, he will honor you with Christlike attitudes that will motivate effective sexual behaviors.* God says in Scripture, "I will take away your stubborn heart and give you a new heart and a desire to be faithful. You will have only pure thoughts, because I will put my Spirit in you and make you eager to obey my laws and teachings" (Ezekiel 36:26–27 CEV). God's transformation of your heart will create a radical empowering as you ask God to grow your desires into his desires.

Third, a heart motivated from God's heart will significantly impact your *behaviors*. As you cultivate a more intimate relationship with God and become more intentional about conforming your heart to his, you will be more successful at creating godly sexual behaviors and more intentional about wise choices from your renewed heart. You'll begin thinking with your heart, soul, and mind rather than being led only by your hormones, emotions, and selfish desires. You will become better at recognizing sinful and immature behaviors that keep you from God's best. This is the essence of growing in sexual maturity and wholeness.

In applying this inside-out approach, consider the truth that God is love (the center "God" circle). What do we know about love from Scripture? Love is patient and kind, not rude or self-seeking (1 Corinthians 13:4–5). Prayerfully seek, then, to intentionally clothe yourself with such traits in your daily interactions with the opposite sex (the middle "heart and attitude" circle), especially if you are currently in a coupling relationship. Begin learning how to put this "love" principle into practice. Think of two or three specific behaviors that would likely be transformed by such a commitment (the outer "behaviors" circle).

Inside-out living requires more work than simply banning behaviors, but it also leads to greater internal motivation and a deeper level of maturity. Let's now apply the inside-out approach to an actual sexual behavior.

What about Masturbation?

What's a conversation about sexuality and single adults without addressing masturbation? For Christians, this remains one of the most frequent and complex issues. Be honest with yourself: how much guilt and anxiety have you expended wondering whether this behavior is "right" or "wrong"?

Martha, a single adult in her late thirties, masturbates a time or two a month. She says it takes the edge off her sexual desire and helps her control lust. Jim, a single in his twenties, believes that stopping masturbation has helped him find greater spiritual perspective and has driven him to deeper intimacy with God and others. Carl thinks the behavior is truly sinful and has a variety of Scriptures supporting his belief.

A quick review of Christian literature over the past three decades reveals that pastors, theologians, and Christian authors have very diverse opinions on the matter. A major factor in this range of opinion is Scripture's silence on the subject. We do find Old Testament laws (Leviticus 15, for example) requiring a person who experienced a "discharge" of semen to be *ceremonially* unclean until evening (the ceremonial laws were, in part, a sobering external reminder of how their *hearts* were to be set apart when they approached God in worship). Another passage (Genesis 38:1–10) references a man named Onan's refusal to consummate his marriage to his deceased brother's wife. According to Hebrew custom, if a man died before having children, his brother was expected to marry the widow and have children by her to carry on the deceased brother's family line. Onan selfishly didn't want to split his inheritance between two households (that of his brother's wife and that of his own wife). Therefore, he attempted to resolve his conflict by practicing *coitus interruptus*—withdrawal of the penis from the vagina prior to ejaculation—and "spilled his seed on the ground" in an effort to prevent having children by her.

So neither of these passages is really about masturbation. *In fact, no Scripture directly deals with the topic.* This is where an inside-out way of thinking proves helpful toward creating a "theology of masturbation."

I remember one time wondering what it would be like to travel back in time and have my own conversation with Jesus about God's perspective on masturbation. I've studied Christ's interactions with people in his earthly ministry and how he often cut to the heart of the matter. One day, God used the following hypothetical dialogue to bring me to a different perspective:

> "Teacher, what do you think about masturbation? Is it always wrong or does it depend?"
>
> "Friend, why do you Christian leaders waste so much time debating masturbation when Satan's deceptions are destroying my gift of sexuality? Have you considered the hypocrisy of your Christian culture?"
>
> "Uh, well . . . the Christian culture does contain distortions. I think maybe we debate masturbation because it creates such guilt for so many."
>
> "Oh, child, what does masturbation mean to you? How does it affect your heart and your relationships?"
>
> "Master, I was thinking a bit more philosophically, trying to develop a theology of masturbation for your Church. Goodness, why do you always get so personal? Now I won't be able to go and tell other Christians *exactly* what to do."
>
> "But *your* heart—*that's* what matters."

We could endlessly debate the subject of masturbation. But here's the place we must start: each believer must go deeper to seek and discern God's heart from the inside out.

The Three-Step Inside-Out Model Applied to Masturbation

How do we synchronize our hearts with God's, applying heart-directed motivation to produce godly behaviors? Whether considering masturbation, fantasy, or any other sexual concern, we'd like to suggest a three-step process that may help you develop an appropriate heart attitude from God's heart in Scripture:

> *Step One:* If scriptural guidelines exist that *directly* address the topic of interest, seek to understand them fully and obediently apply them to your heart, mind, and behaviors. Heart-directed morality always begins with obedience to clear teaching.
>
> *Step Two:* If direct scriptural guidelines do not exist, seek to understand and obediently apply passages that indirectly address the behavior or that support any guidelines you found from step one. Since Scripture often doesn't directly address a specific behavior, we need to explore God's economy through other scriptural principles to guide our hearts and behaviors.
>
> *Step Three:* For topics that are still unclear after applying steps one and two, each believer should prayerfully determine his or her own heart about the issue. God has a sexual economy that works, and he will help you discover his will—however, *you must act on what you already know* as you build godly attitudes and behaviors: "I hope all of you who are mature Christians will agree on these things. If you disagree on some point, I believe God will make it plain to you. *But we must be sure to obey the truth we have learned already*" (Philippians 3:15-16 NLT, emphasis added).

Applying these three steps to the issue of masturbation, we've already discovered that no passages address the issue directly (step one). What about indirectly (step two)? We've listed below a number of passages that seem applicable. After each, we've posed some questions you will want to ask yourself that may lead you toward a personal theology of masturbation.

> *Matthew 5:27-28*—"Anyone who even looks at a woman with lust in his eye has already committed adultery with her in his heart" (NLT). Is the behavior tied to lust? In other words, is the behavior associated with an adulterous or covetous fantasy about someone who isn't currently your spouse? If so, it's inappropriate. See also Job 31:1.
>
> *1 Corinthians 6:12*—"Even though 'I am allowed to do anything,' I must not become a slave to anything" (NLT).

Are you becoming enslaved by or addicted to the behavior, preventing true intimacy? If so, it's spiritually harmful for you.

Philippians 2:4—"Each of you should look not only to your own interests, but also to the interests of others." Is the behavior disrespectful to your future mate, to your future marriage, or to others? Is it self-focused or selfishly gratifying needs that should be met elsewhere? If so, it's inappropriate.

1 Corinthians 6:12—"Not everything is good for you" (NLT). How is this behavior beneficial? How does it affect your growth in Christ?

Genesis 2:24—"This explains why a man leaves his father and mother and is joined to his wife, and the two are united into one" (NLT; see also vv. 18–25). Erotic sexual behaviors should *promote* intimacy and move you *toward* risking healthy intimate relationships and potential marital union. Is the behavior detracting from God's intent? If so, it's not beneficial for you.

Romans 14:14, 23—"But if a person believes something is wrong, that thing is wrong *for him*" (NCV, emphasis added). Do you believe in your heart this behavior is wrong? Is "true" guilt associated with it? (This is different from "false" guilt, which can result from harmful teaching, immaturity, or abuse.) Pay attention to those catches in your spirit about sexual behaviors. *For you*, these may have become inappropriate and harmful.

Romans 14:13 (see also vv. 14–22)—"Make up your mind not to put any stumbling block or obstacle in your brother's way." Is your freedom causing another brother or sister to stumble in his or her faith? If so, then it's at least inappropriate for you to discuss the freedoms you feel regarding this behavior with others who do not feel the same freedom (see v. 22).

By careful searching of Scripture, you may find other passages to assist you in determining a godly perspective about masturbation as well as other sexual behaviors, such as fantasy and flirting (e.g., Matthew 5:28 warns of contaminating potential relationships with lust, and 1 Thessalonians 4:6 warns against wronging another and taking advantage of him or her). By prayerfully allowing Scripture to reveal the deeper purposes of God's heart where no clear guidelines are given on a particular behavior, you may find the Holy Spirit will give you conviction about the issue—not by the *letter* of the law but by the *spirit* of the law. If your heart is truly intent on pleasing God's heart, you will receive wisdom according to God's promise from James 1:5: "If any of you lacks wisdom, he should ask God, who gives generously to all without finding fault, and it will be given to him."

We believe that by working through these and similar questions, you may find masturbation to be an unhealthy attempt to comfort yourself or to deal with some negative emotion by being less than honest with yourself about the *real* issue (such as loneliness, fear, grief, or boredom). God did not intend for us to resolve non-sexual issues through sexual behaviors, like the young man who masturbates himself to sleep every night or the young woman who masturbates to fantasies of men who find her desirable.

Learn to deal with the real issues in healthy ways that actually address the real problems, and stop turning to masturbation for a quick fix. *Sexual activity should never be a substitute for emotional or spiritual intimacy.* Ask God to help you seek diligently the deeper needs of your soul—intimacy with God and close Christian friends—rather than the quick fix of erotic behavior.

Some of you will find masturbation to be outright sinful and totally counterproductive because it's characterized by lustful fantasy, addictive compulsion, and isolation. This type of masturbation will build habits and types of arousal that tear at the foundation of great marital sexual intimacy. For you, to continue with masturbation will actually lead you toward greater sexual distortion, both in your heart now and potentially in your behavior in a future marital relationship. Remember, masturbation is also a heart thing, not just a behavior.

However, some of you (like Martha from earlier in this chapter), may feel that your own masturbation doesn't violate the heart of the Scriptures we shared. For you, masturbation and solo orgasms may simply represent a legitimate means of dealing with sexual surges and hormonal buildup. If so, please remember that *all erotic sexual behaviors merely reflect true sex and will always be incomplete apart from covenant lovemaking in marriage.* Though the physical part of your sexual desire may be lessened, your inner longing for intimacy will remain and should not be ignored.

Even if this is so, always remember to continually discipline your fantasies and guard your thought life from ungodly lust. Actually, your fantasies should come under the same inside-out heart process as do other sexual behaviors. Your eyes, imagination, and thought life play an important role in your sexuality and relationship building with the opposite sex: "The eye is the lamp of the body. If your eyes are good, your whole body will be full of light" (Matthew 6:22).

Incidentally, pornography in its various forms has become *the* rampant disease and vice for the average Christian. As a single adult in a high-tech culture, I (Michael Todd) have had to honestly address this issue in my own Christian walk. Although the Church has begun dealing with this problem better as of late, as sex therapists we fear it is still woefully inadequate. The real moral issue with pornography is the underlying lust and inappropriate fantasy that completely distort and dishonor God's ideal for true sexual intimacy. This is what's sinful, unhealthy, and in need of surrender to God.

In some ways, the medium actually used (magazines, movies, soap operas, trashy romance novels, sexually oriented chat rooms) merely represents the type of "delivery vehicle" for the erotic stimuli. By way of analogy, there are lots of foods that have little to no nutritional value, each being more or less enticing to certain people's tastes. But the type of food doesn't really matter because it's all junk!

We encourage you to address the *deeper heart issues of pornography* that seek to entice and enslave you through all your various senses, whether it be "visual" porn (magazines, movies, strip clubs, soap operas), "audio" porn (phone sex, trashy romance novels, sexually oriented chat rooms), or "mental" porn (the kind where you recall any variety of inappropriate erotic stimuli from the seemingly limitless supply in your own mind and imagination). The type of pornography doesn't matter; your heart does: "Above all else, guard your heart, for it is the wellspring of life" (Proverbs 4:23).

On the flip side, if you don't use your mental imagery and fantasy to create inappropriate lust or to treat your brother or sister as an object of selfish sexual gratification, it's possible for fantasy to actually enhance your relationships by becoming a healthy means of enjoying your sexual identity. "The mind of sinful man is death, but the mind controlled by the Spirit is life and peace" (Romans 8:6). But always remember to "take captive every thought to make it obedient to Christ" (2 Corinthians 10:5).

Our intention is not to judge your hearts. Whatever you decide, we urge you to get on your knees before the Lord to determine what masturbation (and other erotic behaviors) means to your heart—then stand secure in your own relationship with God: "Accept him whose faith is weak, *without passing judgment on disputable matters.* One man's faith allows him to eat everything, but another man, whose faith is weak, eats only vegetables. The man who eats everything must not look down on him who does not, and the man who does not eat everything must not condemn the man who does, for God has accepted him. *Who are you to judge someone else's servant? To his own master he stands or falls. And he will stand, for the Lord is able to make him stand*" (Romans 14:1–4, emphasis added). Be proactive about building a healthy foundation in your own heart and behavior in order to protect fulfilling sexual connection in a potential future marriage.

We know you may find frustrating our lack of laying down specific rules and prohibitions around certain behaviors (except where Scripture is definitive, of course). But being a mature adult in Christ is a *soul* thing, with your sexuality truly being more about who you are than about what you do. However, because behaviors are also important to the life of faith, we have devoted chapter 14 to more specifically addressing common behavior issues within the context of Coupling.

The Heart and Soul of the Matter

Live boldly from your heart! Let your spirit life develop from the inside out, allowing God's love and wisdom to permeate your attitudes and to create meaningful and intimate sexual behaviors consistent with God's heart. "And this is my prayer: that your love may abound more and more in knowledge and depth of insight, *so that you may be able to discern what is best*" (Philippians 1:9–10, emphasis added).

One word of caution: connecting deeply with God's heart and living boldly from your own will place you squarely counter to the culture. In fact, you will be required to take a candid look at a word our culture tends to ridicule: *virginity*. Not only will you need to clarify more honestly the concept of physical virginity, you must also come to terms with the idea that *true* virginity also encompasses your very soul.

Four

The Romance of
Soul Virginity

Principle:
Virginity should encompass body, soul, _and_ spirit

Cassandra views herself as technically a virgin. She's had sexual intercourse with two of her past boyfriends, but neither ever fully made love to her and ejaculated in her vagina. Jimmy knows he's a virgin. He's never kissed or even intimately held his girlfriend, fearing the power of his sex drive and not wanting to take advantage of her. Mark and Tiffany have gone further sexually than either intended. They've been totally nude and created mutual orgasms but congratulate themselves on never having had intercourse. Kristi battles huge guilt over her sexual past and wonders why _any_ Christian guy would want to marry her. Her friend Jenny, influenced by pop culture, "doesn't see why virginity is that big a deal, anyway."

What do all these single adults have in common? They have little idea what virginity is really all about. Like so many singles, they've failed to understand God's loving design for creating and protecting true sexual intimacy through soul virginity. This chapter will unpack the complex but critical topic of virginity—going beyond just the physical to help you understand the deeper truth of this very spiritual concept.

The many viewpoints about virginity are actually quite fascinating. Many singles growing up in the post-sexual revolution eighties and nineties view virginity as old-fashioned. To many, having sex is a sort of teenage rite of passage. Others see it as a standard to maintain, passed on from their parents or church. As with most rules, some singles may be skeptical and wonder if the guidelines aren't imposed to limit fun and personal curiosity—or perhaps are just the "religious" method for birth control or prevention of STDs.

Others are just plain confused. I remember one young couple who maintained their physical virginity but were upset when friends accused them of making a big mistake. What if they were sexually incompatible? Shouldn't they find out before getting married? I looked at the young man and asked, "Do you have a penis?" "Yes," he stammered, surprised at such a direct question. So I asked the young woman, "Do you have a vagina?" to which she replied, "Yes." I reassured them they *were* physically compatible and that true sexual compatibility was built into their hearts and minds rather than into the size, shape, or utility of their plumbing.

Some deeply believe God desires "true love to wait" but are unable to give a *rational explanation* for their virginity. How sad. For humans to experience passionate intimacy as God intended, we must come to realize virginity as the very heart of God's sexual economy. But to gain a better appreciation for this concept, let's first take a brief look at biblical history.

The Old Testament Significance of Virginity

The Old Testament placed a high importance on virginity. The Mosaic law contained severe penalties for men and women who failed to respect marital fidelity (see Deuteronomy 22:13–21). In practical ways, virginity was important because it guaranteed against disease and against children born out of wedlock. Of even greater importance was its representation of personal and relational purity—God's best. Sexual union had been reserved or "set aside" for a particular future purpose. It had not and would not be used for anyone else other than its intended recipient.

The two predominant Hebrew words for "virgin" in the Old Testament are derived from root words meaning "to separate" or "to hide." To separate or hide something was to set it apart as special, unique, valuable—intentionally saved for a particular purpose. God created our sexuality with profound purpose and potential for creating intimacy. The process of separating or hiding was intended to protect and honor its value, much like hiding precious jewelry in a vault. The veils "hiding" the faces of Hebrew women were worn publicly, in part to symbolize this protected status and her inaccessibility to all but her husband (whether present or future).

54

Our culture's idea of virginity is vastly different. It places a premium on the free expression of erotic love. A virgin is someone who at best "hasn't scored yet" or at worst is an outright social outcast (remember the movie *The 40-Year-Old Virgin*?). The Church sometimes doesn't help single adults much in this area either. Though it may teach abstinence, singles often aren't taught *how* or *why* they should wait based on God's sexual economy.

Virginity with "Attitude"

Virginity is really more a soul attitude of faithfully waiting for a covenant companion than about having "had sex" or not. Remember, our sexuality is more about who we are than what we do. *The reason "true love" waits and chooses purity is really quite simple: we wait because we value our sexuality and want to enjoy this awesome expression of intimacy in the context for which God designed it.* We choose to wait for our Adam or Eve and "hide away" aspects of our erotic sexuality for a relationship where such intimate behavior is special and reserved only for that person. As singles, this frees us to focus on pursuing rich *Connecting* with the opposite sex, growing a few of these relationships into mature *Coupling* and perhaps one of them (in time) into the fulfilling marital relationship of *Covenanting*.

Your attitude really does matter. If all you do is try to restrict the physical behavior of intercourse and call that "virginity," you'll likely end up with one of the two extremes of legalistic repression or Christian hedonism, as we discussed in chapter 3. Both miss God's heart for purity and fidelity. Remember our definition of soul virginity:

A **soul virgin** is one who continuously seeks to value, celebrate, and protect God's design for sexuality—body, soul, and spirit—in oneself and others.

We fear for singles who hold physical virginity as "the ultimate goal." How unproductive and hurtful this can be. Instead, the goal should be to build a Christlike character that seeks sexual wholeness and celebrates deep, fulfilling intimacy appropriate to each type of relationship (Connecting,

Virginity ≠ Purity

Coupling, Covenanting). Virginity is the overall lifestyle attitude that guides and protects you along your journey. Physical virginity is a means to the end goal (soul virginity) but is *not* the end itself. It should never be seen as some magical formula for ensuring sexual purity.

I remember the young man who once asked me what "monogamy" meant. I soon discovered his question was more a commentary on his lifestyle than on his vocabulary. I explained that monogamy meant being a "one man" or "one woman" person, exclusively committed to one mate for a lifetime of faithfulness. He looked at me with amazement and asked, "You mean, with millions of women out there, God won't even let me sample four or five before settling down?" I replied, "No, not even two or three. That's just not consistent with God's design for his gift of sex."

Waiting for Our Adam or Eve

To illustrate the importance of soul virginity, consider Jason and Courtney in light of their journey along the Relationship Continuum Bridge. In the process of "confirming" their coupling relationship, they decide to take a day trip to fully disclose their pasts and to discuss their expectations for possible marriage. They've truly enjoyed each other as a couple, but during this time Jason discloses something deep within his heart: he senses God calling him into full-time ministry overseas. After prayerful thought, Courtney doesn't sense this same call for herself, and the two eventually realize their paths are heading in different directions. They decide to do the emotionally difficult work of returning to a connecting relationship. A few years later, Courtney meets Bill and they become engaged.

In a mature and godly manner, Jason and Courtney treated each other as soul virgins—even during their greater commitment in Coupling. Each respected that the other might not be his or her Adam or Eve. They cuddled and enjoyed some erotic behaviors while limiting others, including respecting the godly limit of saving true sex for marriage. Out of a concerned heart for the other, they helped each other grow in maturity throughout their relationship. *Knowing this, Bill sought out Jason and invited him to their wedding.* He genuinely thanked

Jason for his contribution to Courtney's life. Bill expressed appreciation that she was a more whole woman in her femininity and sexuality for having dated Jason. Jason had been an unselfish and courageous man after God's own heart.

Jason, Courtney, and Bill did not allow the opinions of others to define the value of their sexual selves and their pursuit of soul virginity. If you tie your sexual self-worth and behaviors to the vacillating opinions of other people or the culture, your emotions and relationships are in for one scary, unfulfilling roller-coaster ride. Instead, we should *allow God to establish our value* because he made us. As our Creator, he has the right to tell us just what we're really worth.

What, then, is *his* appraisal of your worth? He was willing to pay the price of his own Son's death on an executioner's cross to pay for your sin so you might have an intimate relationship with him. That's the value God places on you. *If you truly see how precious and valuable a treasure you and your sexuality are to him, it will transform the way you allow others to treat you —"significant others" included.*

The Value of Stewardship

Jason understood Courtney's sexual value as a woman created in the image of God. He also recognized the importance of *stewarding relationships.* You may remember the story from Matthew 25:14–30 about the servants who were given various amounts of money to carefully manage and invest while their master was away on business. Each would be individually held accountable for the outcome of their investing upon his return. From this parable flow three truths regarding our role in God's purpose for our lives and our sexuality:

1. God created everything and has graciously *entrusted* things to us for his own good pleasure.
2. Therefore, God is the *owner* of everything, making us the *stewards* of his possessions *for a time.*
3. God's desire is for us to someday return his possessions back to him, having wisely grown them into their true potential—more developed and matured than when they were first entrusted to us.

The teaching of this passage uses the example of money. But the parable certainly applies to other things we are given by God to steward: possessions, time, relationships—and our sexuality. We belong to God and have been bought at a price (see 1 Corinthians 6:20). Our sexuality was certainly a part of the deal. We are privileged to steward it during this short span we call life. *Our hormonal desires, sexual organs, emotional longings—indeed, all of our sexuality—belong to God.*

In God's economy, he has graciously made provision for us to steward and share our sexuality—in the right context. God desires us to steward and develop another person's true sexual potential as Jason did with Courtney. In each relationship along the Relationship Continuum Bridge, true sex—which at least includes sexual intercourse and mutual orgasms—is intended for that final relationship: Covenanting, the one-flesh marital union. The reason? Our sexuality was designed to be the greatest parable of the ultimate love story—God's great love for us (see Ephesians 5:21–33). Sexual intercourse between husband and wife is to reflect God's love for us—pure, priceless, and protected from all who seek to destroy it.

Can you see the bigger picture of why God created sexuality for us to steward and develop? He wants to show us, his valued creation, the importance of love and intimate relationships. Much more is at stake here than just horny feelings, recreational sex, or "falling in love." *God designed our love stories to tell his love story.* It's the love story of all love stories: the God of the universe pursues his creation with white-hot passion and desires a genuine love relationship with each one of us. It's a love story that makes every trashy human romance novel pale by comparison.

How should this affect our view about sexuality? In both relationships (ours with a potential mate and God's with us), faithfulness to the other is the cornerstone. In a spiritual sense, we are engaged to Christ. He asks us to remain faithful to him until he returns for the "wedding feast" (see Matthew 22:1–14; Revelation 19:6–9). *If human marriage is to be a living parable of this, every single adult—assuming he or she will someday marry —should faithfully wait for their future soul mate in a similar manner.*

As single adults, many of you are waiting for your Adam or Eve to complete your own wonderful and unique love story. How you live your life sexually directly impacts the quality of the parable you are portraying about God's love to a lost and dying world—a world desperate for real intimacy. This is why soul virginity matters and why sexual infidelity tears at the very fabric of the gospel message itself.

The truth is, the life you live *does* tell some version of his love story. Will you tell it faithfully by the way you choose to live your life sexually? Will you deeply embrace his love story? These become the haunting questions.

Physical Virginity and Soul Virginity

Physical virginity is the ultimate expression of soul virginity; yet you can still choose to live as a soul virgin even after losing your physical virginity. In chapter 2, we talked about how inadequate the existing language is for expressing and defining single adult sexuality. We have observed with amusement (and sometimes alarm) the terms some singles use for reclaiming and redeeming lost physical virginity. Perhaps a favorite is the term "recycled virgin." We suppose what they mean by "recycled" is the concept of refining something and taking the impurities out, utilizing some of the original materials to make an object useful again.

I had someone as a client once wanting to become a "reconstituted virgin." I tried not to laugh as I inquired what he meant. He said, "You know, I've had sex and I want to follow God's teachings now." Others call it "born-again virginity" or may distinguish between "primary virginity" (no sexual intercourse) and "secondary virginity" (choosing to now abstain after previously being sexually active). Somehow that kind of language seems to lend itself to a rather unfortunate class system: "I'm a primary virgin, but you are only a secondary virgin."

Don't misunderstand us here: giving yourself to a future mate as a physical virgin more closely follows God's plan. It also creates a marvelous intimacy-enhancing gift to your marriage and to your life partner. But regardless of whether you are a physical virgin or not, you can commit to soul virginity by choosing to "hide" or "separate" the more intimate expressions of your erotic sexual behaviors (true sex) from this point forward. This process will also practically serve to re create and restore your sense of sexual worth and integrity.

Virginity is ultimately a heart attitude of chastity and purity. This is why we coined the term soul virgin.

Many of the Old Testament patriarchs made vows to the Lord and frequently created monuments by which to remember such vows. These monuments would also serve to hold them accountable to those vows. In a similar manner, you may need to place such a "monument" at a point in time when making a pledge of soul virginity: "I vow before God from this point forward to not give away my gift of true sex until marriage to my spouse or my marriage to Christ, whichever comes first." This waiting for marriage can become a deep commitment to soul virginity. Perhaps wearing a symbolic monument, such as a ring or bracelet, may help you remember your vow and hold you accountable when you are tempted to forget. Involving friends to encourage, pray for you, and hold you accountable will also help cement the vow.

Incidentally, married people can be soul virgins, too. Once married, the vow of a soul virgin requires the exact same attitude and may be expressed something like this: "I vow before God from this point forward not to give away my gift of true sex to anyone other than my spouse until 'death do us part' or my marriage to Christ, whichever comes first." My wife, Catherine, and I are each other's soul virgins. We have vowed to remain faithful to each other until the end of our lives together on this earth. By contrast, I (Michael Todd) have vowed my soul virginity to a future spouse I have yet to meet. So no matter your marital status, making such a vow is to pursue sexual wholeness by choosing the life of a soul virgin.

What If I'm No Longer a Physical Virgin?

Just because you aren't physically a virgin anymore isn't a cause for despair, though it is an occasion for humble surrender to your heavenly Father with appropriate remorse and lifestyle change. If this is your situation and you find yourself plagued by guilt from your past, we encourage you to hang with us until chapter 5. God's emergency room is open for you, and there you'll find hope and healing in the hands of the Great Physician.

But such a visit to the ER—which will require humility, repentance, and a transformation of your behavior and attitudes from the inside out—will not only restore you to health as a soul virgin but will also restore your sexual integrity. You can become "separated" and "hidden" once again with a renewed dedication to reserve true sex for your future mate. Though the consequences (STDs, sadness, lack of physical virginity, etc.) might remain, *remember that no sexual sin exists that God cannot forgive.* If you seek the Lord, he *will* restore your soul virginity (see 2 Chronicles 7:14).

A brief word of caution to those who are Coupling and are currently sexually active: as you choose to become soul virgins, be careful not to simply repress your sexual behavior. Instead, continue enjoying your relationship while wisely disciplining your sexual desires and erotic sexual behaviors. Alter your lifestyle to support godly changes—but don't stop *all* romantic and erotic relating. We've worked with many couples who completely "turned off" their sexuality during Coupling only to later encounter great difficulty "turning it back on" in marriage (see chapters 14 and 15 for practical helps in this area).

Although previously sexually active together, Jack and Bridget resolved not to share true sex during the last six months of their engagement. Rather than avoiding the temptation, they chose to still spend the nights together. Jack said he "willed himself" to avoid arousal and acting out on his desires. Bridget had to become overly careful to never arouse Jack. Both basically became asexual to ensure they made it to their honeymoon night without having sexual intercourse. They came in for counseling several months into their marriage, fearfully revealing they couldn't reclaim their erotic desire and sexual lovemaking. Together, we had to work through both their repression and the scars from their repression (which they *thought* was soul virginity) as they discovered sexual intimacy within God's economy.

The Cost of Soul Virginity

Some single adults might say, "I can't become a soul virgin. It's too difficult." It *is* difficult . . . and costly, especially for those who have already awakened their more intimate expressions of erotic sexuality in prior romantic relationships. However, making such a commitment will make your sexuality all the more special—both for you and for your future mate.

Soul virgins are rewarded by the deeply abiding presence of Almighty God in their lives and are fulfilled by a level of intimacy with him that leaves others shaking their heads in confusion. *Soul virgins choose to look beyond the here and now to the greater purposes of God for their lives.* They live by enduring principles much bigger than they are—principles that God himself established for his children. Others simply have no frame of reference, for their world does not revolve around Christ and true intimacy. That's the difference.

Dear reader, God will honor your pledge to honor him by living the life of a soul virgin. He understands the sexual ache you feel, with its strong surges of desire and deep longing for intimacy. The Lord himself will meet you in the midst of your struggle for sexual purity with a precious intimate relationship with him that can sustain you through painful times. By relying on his power within you—as you submit to his plan and his authority over your life—you will retain your soul virginity, and the intimacy you experience with God will be greatly rewarding.

The Rewards of Soul Virginity

If you are a Christian who desires to live a God-pleasing life in all your relationships, we strongly commend to you this idea of soul virginity. Take a moment to consider just some of the benefits of living as a soul virgin:

1. You avoid false intimacy, addictions, the seeking of bigger buzzes, and the viruses that demolish sexual wholeness (see chapter 13 for a discussion of the common viruses of soul virginity).
2. You enter coupling relationships without concern about when you'll have sexual intercourse, and you never wake up the next morning wondering what you've done.
3. You attend social gatherings and interact with the opposite sex to create meaningful connecting friendships rather than to scope out the hotties as potential sexual partners.
4. You treat the opposite sex with respect as brothers and sisters in Christ, seeking to build them up in affirming ways. You create valuable connecting relationships that

enhance your sexuality—free of messy, erotic entanglements. You can genuinely enjoy three-dimensional relationships that include body, soul, *and* spirit.

5. You relate with former coupling partners with respect and joy—free of shame and embarrassment.

6. You have a greater appreciation for God's sexual economy and what sexuality is really about. You better understand intimacy and have a healthier respect for sexual surges in ways those who have indulged their desires never will (more on this in chapter 9).

7. You are able to enjoy well-rounded relationships that are not overly dependent on the sexual or romantic aspects but that have evolved the social, spiritual, and emotional aspects as well. You are less likely to ride your sexual feelings into a bad marriage with flaws disguised under the cloak of sexual passion.

8. God becomes more intimate to you as he helps you discipline your sexuality and build the love relationship he desires. Christ, your ultimate bridegroom, takes on a new and deeper meaning in your life.

9. You enter marriage with greater sexual wholeness, less baggage, and a beautiful gift to give to your partner.

10. You have a matured ability to avoid extramarital affairs in your future marriage because you understand the concept of fidelity and have learned to discipline sexual surges. (Incidentally, an amazing number of young couples struggle with affairs in the early years of marriage because they never embraced the deeper concept of covenant faithfulness.)

Valuing your soul virginity and protecting it for your future spouse is a high calling from the Lord. And on your wedding night, should God someday bring a spouse into your life, you will enjoy awesome intimacy and be able to say with all honesty and integrity, "I choose to give you something that has cost me deeply—a very valuable gift—my soul virginity, hidden away just for you."

Even if God chooses not to bring that person along your path, at the end of your days you will stand before your heavenly husband—Jesus Christ—who died on the cross for your redemption. On that day, you can offer to *him* your soul virginity, your precious celibacy, and say these same words with a passion few can repeat: "I choose to give you something that has cost me deeply—a very valuable gift—my soul virginity, hidden away just for you."

You can rest assured he will fully appreciate your gift. He is painfully acquainted with costly gifts. Perhaps that's what makes him such a Great Physician.

Five

God's Sexual Emergency Room

Shame, Guilt, and the Healing Power of Forgiveness

Principle:
Redeem soul virginity through restoration and forgiveness of self and others

Suppose you woke up one morning and said to yourself, "Today I'd like to make some people uncomfortable and watch their faces react with shock and disgust." Here are a couple of easy ways to accomplish that: confess a sexual sin to a friend, or admit that you were sexually abused.

Josh felt his church was more likely to forgive and accept him if he told them he'd killed someone in a fit of rage than if he told them about his struggle with homosexuality. Katie slept with multiple guys in college, was date raped, and had an abortion. Jeanie and Tim are close friends. Both were molested by their moms' boyfriends. Jordan fights sexual addictions and the urge to expose himself. April entered her marriage two months pregnant. How tragic that mistakes and sexual brokenness create such strong reactions of judgment, condemnation, and confusion among Christians—the very group Christ commissioned to reach out to the lonely and broken with a message of hope and healing.

Christian sex therapist and best-selling author Cliff Penner once told me in a personal conversation that he views single sexuality as a hand grenade in the Church—mostly ignored but ready to explode. Guilt runs rampant. Such an inconsistency exists between *stated* Christian values and *actual* Christian behaviors. Penner fears much single adult leadership is lost due to sexual guilt and the inability of the Church to effectively address erotic desires and sexual sin.

In the story of the prodigal son, the father embraced the shamed and dirty son while the older brother looked on with judgment (see Luke 15:11–32). Similarly, our heavenly Father's heart grieves over sexual sin and longs for reconciliation. Why is it that sexual sins seem to create a special kind of guilt and shame?

The Uniqueness of Sexual Sins

Perhaps it shouldn't be surprising. Sexuality in general—and sexual sins in particular—aren't talked about or very well understood within the Christian community. Consequently, they seem scary, shameful, and weirdly perverted. Many in the Church look with disdain on the sexually broken, almost as if they were fearful of being found out themselves. Most Christians don't reflect Christ's compassionate acceptance of the wounded sexual sinner. Jesus wouldn't have flinched or condemned the chronic masturbator, homosexual, adulterer, voyeur, or promiscuous co-ed. He would have gently brought his redemptive touch to bear as he lovingly asked, "Why don't you tell me about it?"

Another reason some people put more weight on sexual sins comes from a misunderstanding of God's sexual economy and redeeming heart in Scripture. Sexual sins indeed touch a part of us few other sins do. *Even the most casual of sinful sexual encounters violates something deep within us:* "Flee from sexual immorality. All other sins a man commits are outside his body, but he who sins sexually sins against his own body. Do you not know that your body is the temple of the Holy Spirit, who is in you, whom you have received from God?" (1 Corinthians 6:18–19).

Our sexuality is core to who we are and expresses the Father's intimate heart. Sexual sins affect us more deeply in their consequences than do lying or being rude to our neighbor. Our sexual sins affect our body, our heart, and our relationships. And often they don't just affect the sinner, as many of you who've been victims of another's sexual brokenness can testify. With sexual sins, God's intimate best is missed. Something that should be especially valued is shared with casual indifference. Promises are broken, beauty is distorted, and trust is betrayed.

Tragically, Christians have confused the *greater consequences of sexual sins with a need for greater disgust and condemnation of those who struggle with such sins. God separates sin and sinner much better than we do.* He doesn't pass out scarlet letters to label you for sleeping with your high school girlfriend, struggling with homosexuality, undergoing an abortion, or having excessive problems with lust or masturbation.

A rewarding part of our ministry as Christian sex therapists is seeing God's restoration of those with sexual sins of significant consequence. Sexual sins aren't less forgivable than other sins. In God's eyes, restoration from such brokenness is merely an opportunity for building a greater monument and testimony to Christ's redemptive power. He graciously invites us to his emergency room for healing.

The Necessity of the ER Experience

Have you ever been to an emergency room? I remember when my ladder (propped up on wet leaves) dropped me ten feet onto a stone walkway. My hand bled profusely, and my bruised ribs made breathing difficult. How glad I was for a place focused exclusively on restoring me to health.

Remember the story of the woman caught in adultery (John 8:1–11)? She also needed a physician of sorts because she was about to die. Fortunately for her, the Physician on duty that day made house calls. He brought the ER to her.

Her story is one of the most captivating passages in all the Gospels. It tells of a woman's miraculous encounter with the Great Physician. She didn't deserve his mercy and care, yet he gave it anyway. Of particular interest is the "prescription" he gave her. Jesus told her accusers they were free to stone her for her sin—but only if *they* were without sin. Of course, none were. One by one, they left the scene. Jesus asked her if any were still condemning her. She answered, "No one."

He then administered his healing antidote: "Then neither do I condemn you. . . . Go now and leave your life of sin" (John

8:11). Jesus prescribed a lifestyle change, a transformation consistent with God's will for her. However, he first performed a "spiritual implant" by giving her the spiritual power necessary to accomplish her behavior change: his forgiveness. "Neither do I condemn you." *Jesus's lack of condemnation would become the spiritual power needed to break through her shame, enabling her to live out God's desire for her. She would have no hope for recovery without it.*

This is what God's sexual ER is all about. When your sexual self becomes distorted or broken, the Great Physician wants to give you a spiritual implant—empowering you through his forgiveness and presence in your life. But you also have your part in this process. Tough choices must be made to focus on healing. You will also need humility to ask others to help you. This isn't always easy. *Time alone doesn't heal, but time with treatment can bring healing, relief from guilt, and restoration.* Surrendering to God and allowing him to perform spiritual surgery his way is vital. You can't undergo this process of redemption alone. Seek out God's emergency room and allow others in the body of Christ to come alongside you on this journey toward healing and restoration.

The ER Treatment

God didn't panic when Adam and Eve forever distorted his beautiful creation. Neither does he do so with us in our sin. Instead, he lovingly makes a way to "bind up the brokenhearted, to proclaim freedom for the captives . . . to comfort all who mourn and provide for those who grieve" (Isaiah 61:1–2). Instead of shame and disgrace, "everlasting joy will be theirs" (v. 7).

When we're wounded and hurting, especially sexually, we can come to God's emergency room. This ER is equipped with the treatment options necessary to heal our distorted and broken sexuality. We must apply God's prescription courageously as we seek healing of intimate relationships and the restoration of soul virginity. Let's look at a few of the more common remedies in the ER. They include grieving, confessing, repenting, forgiving, making amends, and becoming whole.

Grieving

"Blessed are those who mourn, for they shall be comforted" (Matthew 5:4 NKJV). Because we live in a broken world, we must learn to grieve. Grieving can take many forms, but it's often filled with cleansing, healing tears as we work through denial, anger, and hurt. *Although physical tears aren't always necessary, admitting truth, feeling painful feelings, and letting go of things are.* God knew we would need grieving to help heal our souls in this messy world. He promises we will be comforted.

Kyle and April were in God's sexual ER because they were getting married but neither had set effective sexual boundaries in their past romantic relationships, including with each other. They were engaged at the time April got pregnant. Both wanted their marriage to be different than their Coupling. As a result, April began to explore the fears of being abandoned that had motivated her sexual behaviors in the first place. Kyle became honest with himself about his using past girlfriends for his own selfish sexual gratification. Both grieved over what they'd lost over the years as they pushed toward healing. Once April allowed herself to grieve, it wasn't just over what she'd forfeited with Kyle—lots of distorted and hurtful relationships with men came flooding back to her memory, especially her relationship with her dad.

As with April and Kyle, our grieving may be cumulative. The present loss may trigger grief over past losses that have never been properly let go of and healed. Grieving isn't a process that can be worked through totally alone. You will need others to share the process with you, holding and encouraging your wounded soul as it cries tears of release.

True guilt (or godly sorrow) is a catalyst for healthy grief that drives us toward needed change, getting us back to God's way of thinking about our lives. Without it, we'd likely miss out on his best. If we ask the Holy Spirit's guidance to convict us of sin, he will lead us straight to God's emergency room. Such conviction helps us see more clearly where we've violated God's values, motivating us toward healthy grief, confession, and repentance: "For God can use sorrow in our lives to help us turn away from sin and seek salvation" (2 Corinthians 7:10 NLT).

Our emotions can serve us well if we allow them to motivate us toward godly change. Some emotions quickly sour if we hold on to them. Instead, use them as short-term catalysts for change, choosing to see them as God's tools for mending the losses in your broken places. *Anger* can show you that justice has been violated. *Envy* can reveal that something's missing. *Fear* can motivate you to seek help. Some emotions—like love, joy, contentment, and desire—are more long term. These can be cultivated for creating and nurturing intimacy. In God's ER, emotions are used to do their servant function in our minds as well as our hearts. The sooner we understand the purpose for a particular emotion, the sooner we learn what is needed to change and heal.

Confessing

What's your darkest secret? What skeletons are in your closet you desperately hope no one discovers? We could probably guess that for most of you they are sexual. And we wouldn't be surprised if you're still hanging on to them, either. Healing confession of sexual brokenness is a gift we don't often receive in the Church. I remember Jordan, a client who struggled with sexual addiction and exhibitionism. One day we were discussing how great it would be if he could find a mature couple in his church to mentor him. He could tell them, "I'm struggling with exhibitionism," and they would reply, "Dear brother, we're so sorry. That's a tough sin to wrestle with. Tell us more about your struggle, and let us come alongside you and love you toward greater soul virginity."

We then both burst out laughing: "Yeah, right! Do these kind of people even exist?" But believe it or not, they do. Jordan *was* able to find compassionate, godly people to love and accept him. But we won't lie to you. They're not always easy to find.

"People who cover over their sins will not prosper. But if they confess and forsake them, they will receive mercy" (Proverbs 28:13 NLT). What a surprising gift confession becomes for healing guilt and covering a multitude of sins. Confession brings secrets to the light, draining their power. Satan operates in secrecy and darkness. The secrets we hide fester and gain greater destructive power. But when we bring them to the light, God gives us his perspective on them. The person who confesses sinfully lusting after another person often finds the attraction greatly diminished the next time that person crosses his or her path. As we confess our secrets, Satan is robbed of his condemning power—giving us hope and perspective to make necessary changes.

Confession also allows God and another caring person to see our ugliness and *still love us*. In our previous examples, April, Kyle, and Jordan experienced the healing power of confession when they trusted enough to risk revealing their secrets. We can let go of guilt and shame as we separate sin from sinner. We move from imposters to redeemable sinners when someone knows our ugly secrets and *still* loves us. "Confess your trespasses to one another, and pray for one another, that you may be healed" (James 5:16 NKJV).

Confession is a life-changing gift to both the one who is confessing and the one who receives the confession. The one confessing is exposing wounds and ugliness, courageously embracing trust and bravery, revealing the *total* secret, painfully grieving, and accepting of love and care from the one receiving the confession. The one receiving the confession covers the confessor with grace-filled acceptance and forgiveness, wisely practices complete confidentiality and trustworthiness, isn't repulsed by the sinner, and doesn't pass judgment on him or her.

Seeking out appropriate confessors isn't an easy process. Men need other men to hear their *gut-level honest* confession, men who will encourage them and hold their feet to the fire without overreacting. Women need a female buddy with whom they can unload, feel understood, and be exhorted toward growth. Both men and women need safe people in their lives who truly care about them. At times you will need to both give and receive this gift of confession as you mature in your soul virginity.

Repenting

Repentance is a central element in biblical redemption. It demonstrates that we recognize and accept responsibility for our destructive thoughts and behaviors. *We must choose to make necessary changes as God breaks the power of sin and encourages growth in our lives.*

Repentance means putting feet to our remorse, making tough choices to create different sexual attitudes and behaviors.

With the Holy Spirit's empowering and enlightenment, we will "produce fruit in keeping with repentance" (Matthew 3:8) as we mature in soul virginity. Remember, becoming a soul virgin is a *process*.

We know some of you have already encountered serious sexual sin. Please know that God is no more repulsed by you than a doctor receiving a trauma victim in the ER. However, his hatred for your *condition* will motivate him to use his healing touch to mend you back to health. Your presentation in the ER is all that's required.

Katie (whom you met at the beginning of this chapter) was sexually involved with many guys in college. Three of them were casual hookups when she was drunk. She never considered herself promiscuous before her experience in God's ER. But when Christ invaded her life, she felt cheated and ashamed. This godly sorrow began a process of godly character changes in her lifestyle, resulting in her growth toward soul virginity. This will continue to require many ongoing choices over her lifetime.

We must actively search out the destructive thinking and behaviors that are damaging our sexuality to change them. Making initial changes and then *continuing* to make changes is the only way sexual healing and growth take place. But take heart in Scripture's promise: "The God who started the great work in you [will] keep at it and bring it to a flourishing finish on the very day Christ Jesus appears" (Philippians 1:6 Message).

An important part of sexual repentance is breaking the unseen hold sinful relationships have on an individual. When two people have sex outside of marriage, they become "one flesh" according to Scripture (1 Corinthians 6:16); an intimacy has been established. Here's a practical step many have found helpful: specifically recall each person you've ever shared true sex with, asking forgiveness from God and for him to break any bonds still existing between you. This can serve as an important part of repentance and growth toward reclaiming soul virginity.

Forgiving

Kari came to me weeping that she'd ruined her honeymoon. Though her wedding was still three weeks away, she was not a physical virgin and feared her sexual past had "totally destroyed" any chance of a meaningful honeymoon. I asked if she felt God and her fiancé had forgiven her. She replied that Jeremy had amazed her in his understanding, forgiveness, and acceptance of her. Of course, God had also forgiven her. I helped her understand that her past wasn't going to ruin her honeymoon. It was her false guilt and *inability to forgive herself* that might damage the gift her loving heavenly Father so abundantly wanted to give her in her marriage to Jeremy.

Pardon is a great word for forgiveness. It's the picture of zeroing out the ledger balance, even though you haven't paid the bill. It's keeping a short account by stopping blame or releasing guilt. As Christians, we're not given an option about forgiving: we forgive because we've been forgiven. Jesus taught us to forgive "seventy times seven" (in other words, as many times as it takes), not because our offender deserves it but because we are to remember how great a debt we owed that was canceled by God himself (Matthew 18:21–35). From the divine viewpoint, another person's sin against us is small when compared with our sins against God. Therefore, to not forgive another's offense is to mock God's own gift of forgiveness to us.

But, like Kari, we sometimes find the most difficult person to extend grace to is *ourselves* when we are the offender. Whether for others or ourselves, restoration in God's ER comes by letting go the disease of unforgiveness, allowing God to cleanse us with his healing salve of mercy and pardon.

"The Lord is compassionate and gracious, slow to anger, abounding in love. . . . He does not treat us as our sins deserve" (Psalm 103:8, 10). God knows we desperately need his grace. God's forgiveness enables us to offer the same to others —and to ourselves. We must learn to master forgiveness as one of God's healing arts. Some simple beginning steps might include:

1. Confess your sins to yourself, to God, and to a trusted Christian brother or sister (this could also be a minister, spiritual director, counselor, or accountability partner). Allow this other person to help you separate sin from sinner and to demonstrate to you God's loving acceptance and forgiveness.

2. Thank God for his mercy and forgiveness as you embrace it with your head *and* your heart. Consider praying through Psalm 51 or Psalm 103.

3. Ask God to help you grieve your losses and release the shame so you might see the wonderful "hope and future" he has for you (Jeremiah 29:11).

4. Make needed behavior changes and restitution to clear your conscience and reconcile your relationships.

Making Amends (Restitution)

After his own confession and repentance, Zacchaeus told Jesus he would make amends to those he had cheated as a tax collector: "If I have cheated anybody out of anything, I will pay back four times the amount" (Luke 19:8). Christ saw evidence of true repentance *in his action*. Zacchaeus obviously needed to make these amends to experience deeper healing.

Other words to describe making amends are *restoration* or *restitution*. Making amends is a tool that reinforces your change of heart. It also helps in restoring trust and intimacy in your important relationships, promoting further growth and healing. Kyle and April decided part of their making amends to each other would be prioritizing time and money for counseling. Attending a support group that promotes honesty or offering apologies to those you've offended are examples of direct amends. Mentoring teens in your church so they avoid making your same mistakes would be an example of an indirect amend.

Be careful, though: all amends aren't necessarily healthy and healing. In the Twelve-Step model of recovery, step nine wisely says, "We make direct amends to people where possible, *except when doing so will injure them or others*."[1] It's not just about your need to make things right. To unearth an issue that has been dormant for twenty years or to disclose a hurt previously unknown to the other person isn't always healing.

Seek out a mature friend for advice before undertaking such amends. In some cases, amends may need to be indirect rather than directly to the offended party. Fortunately, vertical reconciliation (seeking forgiveness from and reconciling with God) *doesn't* depend on horizontal reconciliation (seeking relational reconciliation with others).

Becoming Whole

Once our immediate wounds are bandaged, the Great Physician places on us the responsibility for overcoming our immaturity and skill deficits. Put simply, this is about growing up. Reading this book and finding other helpful instruction will go far in overcoming ignorance. *Nurturing our soul virginity is a lifelong process of choices and growth toward maturity.* We must learn these ER skills, especially those of confessing and forgiving. They are neither fun nor easy, but God will help us grow as we master them.

Through some tough maturing time in God's ER, Josh realized that becoming more Christlike was both a godlier and a healthier goal than simply striving to "become straight." His lack of soul virginity was deeper than merely his struggle with same-sex attraction. He needed to better appreciate his masculinity and to heal his mother and father wounds. He recognized his need for making female friends who valued and encouraged his masculinity rather than treating him as "one of the girls." He was also becoming more aware of his struggle with isolation and sexual addiction. His journey toward intimate friendships and soul virginity was a long and difficult process—but worth the effort of growing up.

Our Father's Heart and the Process of Restoration

Do the consequences of your sin haunt you at times? Does every new relationship unearth old memories of sexual brokenness you'd just as soon forget? Like Kari, do you fear you've ruined not only your honeymoon but any hope for meaningful soul virginity? Recall the story of the prodigal son: "So he got up and went to his father. But while he was still a long way off, his father saw him and was filled with compassion for him; he ran to his son, threw his arms around him and kissed him" (Luke 15:20). What he had done didn't repulse his loving father, nor did it diminish the father's love for the son he longed to restore. He desired only to bring his child back into his emergency room for healing and restoration.

Restoring What's Lost

A striking aspect of our Father's heart is revealed in the book of Joel. Israel was often spoken of as a woman who, in her attempts to follow the gods of the nations around her, "played the harlot," spiritually speaking. Scripture frequently records how God disciplined the nation of Israel for her spiritual adultery, either by sending plagues or by allowing a neighboring nation to take her captive and remove her from the Promised Land. But by his mercy—rather than allowing her to remain forever damaged—God would astonishingly promise to restore her losses if only she would exhibit true remorse, confession, and repentance over her sin: "Says the Lord, 'Turn to Me with all your heart, with fasting, with weeping, and with mourning.' So *rend your heart and not your garments.* Return to the Lord your God, for He is gracious and merciful, slow to anger, and of great kindness, and He relents from doing harm. . . . [He says,] '*I will restore to you the years that the swarming locust has eaten*'" (Joel 2:12–13, 25 NKJV, emphasis added).

Of course, some consequences of your past sins may remain, such as an STD, haunting memories, the loss of innocence, the loss of physical virginity, or the death of an aborted child. However, in marvelous ways *restoration can still take place* if you will humbly admit your sinful behavior to your loving Father, abandon it, and return to faithful soul virginity. In so doing: (1) a deeply meaningful love relationship with God can be restored; (2) God will heal your guilt and allow you to live fully in the present rather than continuously grieving the past; (3) he will give you renewed perspective that the past wasn't "totally locust plagued" because his loving presence buffered you from even greater distortion; (4) he will teach you valuable lessons in the midst of your pain; and (5) he will work through such lessons to mature you and prepare you for healthier future relationships.

All the single adults mentioned in this chapter are living testimonies to our heavenly Father's ability to forgive and restore. Their experiences of sexual healing and renewed soul virginity are shared to give you hope.

Dad's Amazing Gift: A Modern-Day Parable

Jane was home from graduate school for her birthday. For her father to be this late was unusual. Although he worked as an ER physician, he should have been home hours before now.

Just then, the front door opened. Her father's eyes twinkled as he carefully placed a magnificently wrapped gift in front of her. Jane eagerly opened the package and discovered to her amazement a sleek laptop computer. She thanked her dad with a big bear hug. It was the best present she'd ever received. The usefulness of the gift made it all the more valuable.

Jane was thrilled with excitement as her dad went over the manual and showed her what the computer could do. She was a bit overwhelmed with the gadgetry of it all; modems, ports, network cards, and lots of other stuff she didn't really understand. But her new laptop had interactive games, searchable Bible software, and an electronic calendar to remind her of deadlines. She could wirelessly surf the Internet, download cool songs, and communicate with everybody. Best of all, she could take it anywhere.

The gift scared her a bit too. She hoped to master its complexities and not mess it up. She wasn't a techno geek like her father, but she could certainly learn. She was amazed how one present seemed to affect her whole existence. She laughed to herself, hoping it wouldn't be like in the movies with the computer taking over the matrix of her life! What an adventure to have so much to discover and enjoy.

Months have passed, and Jane is coming home again from grad school with excitement—along with some embarrassment and shame. Her laptop really has changed her life for the better. She remembers, though, that first heart-wrenching experience when she allowed a friend to install some software. It crashed part of the system and affected the functioning of many programs. She also inadvertently got an email virus that she still isn't sure is fully eliminated. Lots of the computer functions seemed so easy when her dad explained them, but now she feels so confused.

Her father understood both her excitement and her need for help. Despite her guilt and shame, he was very supportive when she told him about her mistakes. "Don't worry, sweetheart," he gently replied. "Just bring the computer home. I'll teach you more about it and restore it like new."

Like Jane's father, our heavenly Father has given us a precious gift. Your sexuality has great capacity for both good and evil, both amazing pleasure and agonizing pain. Through the pages of Scripture, he's given you the manual to help you understand how his gift is best used within the Creator's awesome design. Our prayer is that this book will remind you to consult God's "manual" regularly.

Leaving the ER for the Real World

If you, like the single adults in this chapter, have entered the ER and encountered the Great Physician personally, you can appreciate the spiritual resources he's made available to you. You not only have his instruction for living the life of a soul virgin, you also have the power to break shame and to carry out godly changes through his forgiveness of your past. That power resides in the Holy Spirit, God's own "spiritual implant" inside you.

But here's a thought-provoking question: do you trust the prescriptions he's given you will actually work? Or perhaps this question hits nearer the truth: *do you really trust his heart to restore you "like new"?* If not, you will leave God's ER full of doubts that could shackle you to despair. As we've said before, soul virgins often pay a high price for their godly lifestyle. In the same way eating healthy costs more than eating junk food, so godly living often carries a more expensive price tag. But like with food, those who choose well live well. As you'll soon discover, God has made available everything single adults need to experience fulfilling lives of sexual wholeness.

One Is a Whole Number

Principle:

Single adults *can* **experience fulfilling intimacy**

A young man once told me after attending one of my singles workshops, "You are lucky to be married; you're never lonely and have instantly available sex." I asked him where he got this "instantly available" rule for marriage. I really liked that rule but just wasn't aware of it—and would appreciate it if he would tell my wife!

Here's the truth on never being lonely: ultimately, we're all lonely and alone. However, this is not a curse. Marriage can never be the antidote to loneliness, nor does it create wholeness in the individual. Only a real relationship with God can accomplish this. Each person, married or single, is ultimately alone with God. Yes, God has given us wonderful gifts in the form of marriage and being a part of a larger caring community. But even still, each of us has tremendous opportunity and responsibility to pursue intimate completion with his or her Creator.

Yet doubt remains for many Christian single adults about the purpose of their ongoing singleness: "I can't believe I'm still single in my mid-thirties. What's wrong with me?" "Maybe I need to visit a new singles' group to find Mr. Right." "If God loves me, why am I still single?" "I had sex with my boyfriends before committing to soul virginity. God must be punishing me." While it's possible your singleness may be due in part to a lack of maturity or past choices, our loving heavenly Father doesn't withhold good things from his children to be mean or to punish them and certainly not because of his lack of love for them. He desires to give good gifts to his children (Matthew 7:7–11). Perhaps his desire is to give you an even greater gift.

Finding Contentment (and Even Joy) in the Single Journey

As much as some singles believe it's true, marriage will not meet all your needs. In fact, healthy intimacy doesn't depend on marriage at all. That has been the message of the entire first section of this book. *Meeting your deepest intimacy need does not begin with a mate.*

So if marriage isn't the solution, what is? *Real intimacy begins with the One the parable of marriage was intended to be a reminder of: God himself.* He is the most important source for your intimacy needs and growth toward soul virginity. The second most important source is connection with godly brothers and sisters. Only against the backdrop of these two relationships—God and God's people—can a healthy love life with a spouse grow to maturity as God intended. Said another way, *You must first learn to be a satisfied single adult in order to become a mature and satisfied married adult.*

Maturity in marriage only comes through maturity in singleness—both relationally and sexually. Singles must first learn who they are *independent* of a spouse; otherwise, they will forever be looking to their mate to "complete them." You may remember the movie *Runaway Bride* with Julia Roberts, whose character had a desperate yet fearful desire to be married. Unfortunately, she had a version of this same mistaken idea. Somehow marriage was supposed to meet her deepest needs for love, acceptance, and self-esteem. She jumped from relationship to relationship, conforming to the personality of the other to win his affection—yet without a clue to who she really was within herself. Each potential suitor took her further away from herself—until she met Richard Gere's character, who forced her to look within herself at her own problem.

Marriage is better seen as the *multiplication* of two people together than as the *addition* of two people. In other words, when two "halfway" healthy people come together, it's not $1/2 + 1/2 = 1$. It's more like $1/2 \times 1/2 = 1/4$. God's plan is simple: 1 (whole person) x 1 (whole person) = an amazingly whole one-flesh synergy. *Two whole, grown-up people are needed to make a whole, healthy marriage.* This is especially true in Christian marriage, where each is to seek how to please and serve the other rather than to seek how they can be pleased and served *by* the other.

Growing old is mandatory, but growing up is optional. Both before and during marriage, the "grown-up" person who puts on Christlike maturity (Colossians 3:12–14) and learns to live confidently alone is the one who thrives. Learning selflessness by loving God and serving others in the community of faith are essential training for marriage.

Christian single adults have been duped far too long into believing the lie that romance and erotic sexual behaviors are the only things worth living for. It's about the only message we hear from Nashville and Hollywood—you're of little worth unless you can find that "special someone."

Here's a radical thought: what would happen if you took the desperate energy you spend looking for a mate and instead redirected it into a *desperate seeking after God*? How intimate would your relationship with him become as a result of that kind of investment? You would likely find an intimacy unheard of by most single adults—non-Christian and Christian alike. What a foundation you would build for intimate Coupling with a potential future mate!

A Purpose and a Cause Worth Living For

Single adults can easily get lost in their own frustration and loneliness, losing sight of the bigger picture. Throughout the course of human history, various individuals have risen up from the masses to leave a mark on our lives: inventors, politicians, philosophers, artists, and religious leaders. All had at least one thing in common: they were visionaries who saw beyond themselves. They passionately dedicated their lives to causes greater than their own individual worlds. When people catch a glimpse of something much larger than themselves, something they deeply believe in, seemingly nothing is too difficult for them. They frequently are willing to give their lives for such a cause.

This is the true nature of our relationship with God. John Piper says it this way: "God is most glorified in us when we are most satisfied in Him."[1] Have you ever truly been "satisfied in him" and him alone? The ultimate cause worth living for is falling in love with Christ, either for the first time or coming back to your "first love" all over again (Revelation 2:4). God deeply desires a genuine love relationship with you.

Perhaps you aren't even sure what that looks like. It's crucial to your becoming whole both personally and sexually. We'd like to give you some practical steps for cultivating intimacy with God. Many more ideas could be listed here, but this will at least get you started.

Cultivating a Love Relationship: Letters

Creating a more intimate and fulfilling relationship with God begins with learning about him. What does he care about? What pleases him? What saddens him? With a human lover, one way to express your thoughts and feelings is through love letters. You might write about big things, small things, and everything in between.

In much the same way, God has written many love letters to you in the form of Scripture. The Bible is filled with stories about how God feels on lots of things. It also contains letters of instruction, sharing God's heart about certain matters. There's also an entire section of poetry, much of which reveals God's character. Learning about God is vital to having a relationship with him. How can you have an intimate relationship with someone you don't know that well?

If you're new to studying Scripture, you might try visiting your local Christian bookstore and thumbing through different translations of the Bible for yourself. Dozens of good English translations are available today. The key is finding one you can easily understand. Consider one that includes study notes. While you shouldn't rely upon such notes to the degree you would trust God's inspired Word in Scripture itself, they can often help you better apply God's Word to your everyday life. Ask your minister or the bookstore's manager to help you with this decision.

While you're at it, ask about Bible study material or other Christian literature that can also further your learning. Other ways to grow your love relationship with God might include attending a Bible class at a local church, subscribing to a daily devotional guide, and listening to sermons or praise music on the radio, television, or the Internet. Keeping a personal journal of how the Holy Spirit speaks to you during your study time is a great way to document God's personal activity in your life. Later on, when God seems either silent or difficult to understand, your journal may serve as a tangible reminder of how he has already spoken and worked through you.

Deepening Your Love Relationship: Conversations

Reading Scripture is God's primary way of talking with you; prayer is your primary way of talking with him. Prayer is simply having a conversation with God, much like you would have with another person. What should you talk about? Anything! Whatever is on your heart is a great place to start (see Philippians 4:6). Because of who God is, it's also appropriate to tell him how much he means to you and how much you love certain things about him.

You can thank God not only for who he is but also for the things he's done for you. If something is bothering you, share it with him. If you want to ask him for something, go ahead. If in his wisdom he knows it's a good thing for you, he will certainly provide it in his timing; if it's not, he won't (or he might even provide something better in the long run). After praying, watch to see what happens in your life, and don't forget to thank him for his answers when they come. God is like a loving father with his young child—there's *nothing* in your life he doesn't want to hear about. If it matters to you, it matters to him!

Sometimes a conversation with God doesn't even have to involve an exchange of words. I (Michael Todd) sometimes find my most meaningful times with God are spent in silence and solitude while watching nature from my screen patio. Still your heart and mind, allowing God's Spirit to commune with you in the quiet.

Sharing Your Love Relationship: A Mission

Once you have an understanding of the things God cares about, you can begin investing your time in those things. Service in a local church and other Christian ministries is one of the primary ways this happens. You could serve in many different ways, so you should find ways consistent with the gifts and talents God has given you. Take a "spiritual gifts inventory" or talk with a pastor about ways you might serve best. Or just try some things: play an instrument in the orchestra, work in a preschool Sunday school class, serve at a homeless shelter or clothes closet, participate in visitation or evangelistic outreach, go on a mission trip overseas, or help with a summer youth camp. Whatever you do, remember you are building your love relationship with God as you serve others (Colossians 3:23). You'll be amazed at how reaching out beyond yourself gives you perspective and helps alleviate your loneliness and self-preoccupation.

God and You—A Majority

Remember how we said that ultimately we're all individuals alone with God? Meaning and contentment stem from your relationship with him. God gives us personal responsibility to love and nurture ourselves as we each delight in our individual relationship with him, whether we are single or married. "But each one must examine his own work, and then he will have reason for boasting in regard to himself alone, and not in regard to another" (Galatians 6:4). This personal wholeness gives us the resources necessary for fulfilling intimacy in both friendships and marriage—even adding richness to such relationships.

Love the Skin You're In

Self-esteem ultimately comes from accepting God's decree that you are "fearfully and wonderfully made" (Psalm 139:14), independent of another's opinions about your looks, personality, strengths, and weaknesses. You are special and can be excited about being you. This includes your sexuality, gender, and body image. God has given you a unique song and a special name in which you can take comfort and find joy (Revelation 2:17).

Learn the art of self-affirmation. Create a list of a dozen things you thank God for in the person he created you to be. As you become comfortable in your own skin, forget about yourself and reach out to enjoy friendships in deeper and more meaningful ways. Becoming a soul-sexy man or woman is extremely difficult when you aren't first comfortable in your own skin.

Nurture Yourself

Nurturing yourself and learning to enjoy your own company isn't the same as being self-absorbed. People who can find contentment in being alone make great friends and mates. Encourage variety and novelty in your life; develop an appreciation for hobbies and adventure; cultivate sensuality with flowers, leisurely baths, or art galleries; recreate your body and mind; make yourself relax; take hikes in nature, allowing God to restore your soul beside "quiet waters" (Psalm 23).

Stay Childlike

As adults we tend to forget the natural curiosity and playfulness of childhood. Jesus said we would learn about the kingdom of heaven by observing and imitating children—creatures who possess an awe of the world around them and live to play. Let God inspire the child in you, motivating attitudes and activities that turn your loneliness into daily adventures. Enthusiastically express your feelings. Laugh at yourself. Play games and have fun as you free the child within you.

Create "Spontaneous Structure"

Maturity combines intentional routines with creative spontaneity. "All work and no play makes Jack a dull boy." The paradox is that all play and no work makes Jack an immature boy. Mature people practice *discipline*—deliberate steps for getting enough sleep, eating healthily, and engaging in proper exercise. Cultivating intimacy with God and others demands *disciplined routines and choices*. Yet the Creator also loves *mystery and surprise*, with his love being "new every morning" (Lamentations 3:23). Indulging in surprises and impromptu adventure creates fun and variety in life. David and Peter, men after God's own heart, are biblical examples of spontaneity and passion (2 Samuel 6:12–15 and Matthew 14:25–29, respectively). Contented single adults have a balance of both discipline and spontaneity.

Love Relationships: Filling the Intimacy Vacuum

Perhaps you've noticed that building intimacy with God is much like building intimacy with another person. That's because our human relationships are reflections of our relationship with God. He is by nature a relational being and created us with the same capacity for intimate relationship. We shouldn't be surprised that when Jesus was asked what he considered to be the two greatest commandments, he responded, "Love the Lord your God with all your heart" and "Love your neighbor as yourself" (Mark 12:30–31).

God and God's people—for the Christian single, this is where it all begins. These two relationships *must* represent your greatest investment of time. Having an intimate relationship with God is of highest importance. At the end of the day, it always comes back to being alone with God. What other people think about you doesn't matter if it's not in harmony with your heavenly Father.

However, God knew we would need some representation of him here on earth through which he could love us and demonstrate his presence with us—people who could smile with us when we're happy, cry with us when we're sad, and hold us when we feel lonely or afraid. This is why God encourages us toward *community*—real relationships with men *and* women— with whom he designed us to connect deeply in genuine, non-erotic intimacy (see Hebrews 10:24–25). It's the purpose of the Church, the place where soul virgins gather to develop relationships with others to help meet their need for intimacy.

As you'll see in the following section, we need healthy connecting relationships with both men and women. Connecting is part of God's plan for wholeness. These intimate friendships become basic training for building a mature character and learning the intimacy skills necessary to please a future soul mate.

Part 2:

Intimacy with God's People

Seven

Soul-Sexy
Masculinity

Principle:

God calls men to humble initiative and inner strength

Like many men, I've had an interesting journey growing into my own masculinity. I've had friends tell me, "Doug, there are many things you can be, but *macho* is certainly not one of them." My gentle nature and lack of aggression have troubled me at times. My unusual tenor voice and what my colleagues call my "cute personality" don't strike awe or fear into most people. The other day I was shopping with my wife and the sales clerk called me "adorable." Darn. I was hoping for "dangerous" or "dashing"!

A conversation that helped me become more comfortable in my own skin occurred many years ago with my counseling center administrator. Without any come-on, she told me, "Doug, I know you struggle with your masculinity, but you don't know how sexy *gentle* is to women." Since then, I've reveled in being a sexy, gentle man.

The Complexity of Gender

God chose to reveal himself through gender sexuality—the amazing interplay between masculinity and femininity. Maleness and femaleness, with their complex interactivity, show us insights into the Almighty and his love of mystery and intimacy.

Trying to understand masculinity and femininity surfaces some fascinating and seemingly conflicting ideas: (1) men and women are more alike than they are different, (2) the ways they magnetically attract and intimately complement give us unique insights into our Creator (going way beyond mere biology), and (3) each man and woman possesses at least *some* traits of both masculinity and femininity.

Beware of Stereotypes and Prejudice

All people relate equally as children of God. In our essence as human souls, we're exactly the same: "There is neither . . . male nor female, for you are all one in Christ Jesus" (Galatians 3:28). In our sexuality, personality, and human needs, more similarities exist than differences. We all need God at the center of our universe. He must also be allowed to reign over our sexual desire as it pushes us toward intimate relationships.

In each of us, facets of God's image in masculinity and femininity coexist. My wife, Catherine, makes logical decisions (a traditionally masculine trait), while I decide more often with my feelings (a traditionally feminine trait). Our culture and family backgrounds also affect the manner in which we live out our masculinity or femininity within our male or female gender.

So when a conversation about gender differences and interactions between the genders comes up, try to go beyond simplistic, cliché answers. Our Creator reveals himself through these complex differences. Don't use gender to gain power, manipulate, or put someone in a restrictive box. These differences have nothing to do with status, equality, or worth. The strength and allure of our genders should be enjoyed and celebrated as we utilize them to maximize relationships, not to manipulate or control.

The Harm of Unisex

In recent times, some in our society have attempted to blur the lines between the sexes. Although they may have many possible motives for doing so, we see great risk in denying one's gender and how it interacts with the opposite sex. We're all created male or female with a unique gender identity capable of synergy with others—a wonderful dance to enjoy. Like magnetic fields, we attract and create forces that would not exist apart from gender. The different parts we play create a beautiful musical harmony of vibrating souls. Men come alive from traits women bring out in them, and women feel more secure in the presence of male attention. Even within the Christian community, we sometimes downplay these differences rather than understanding and celebrating them.

Chapters 7 and 8 will explore what it means to be a soul-sexy man or woman. These suggestions won't fit everyone. Create your own unique dance with the opposite sex as you understand and accept your personal gender identity. The "soul-sexy" concept emphasizes that masculinity goes beyond strong bodies, deep voices, or the stereotypes of what's "hot." The qualities of maleness, enjoyed within themselves and in intimate relationships, are more complex and soulful qualities. Being chiseled and strong and having sex appeal doesn't adequately define soul-sexiness for the soul virgin man.

A Chest of Drawers—Traits of Masculinity

Men are like chests of drawers, with separate compartments for everything and nothing very self-disclosing on top. Men tend to be more private and not as self-revealing. They often view life as a competitive arena. Their conversations reveal less information because "knowledge is power, and one must be guarded." They often organize their lives with a work drawer, a "family and friend" drawer, a recreation drawer, and a God drawer. Everything has a separate space, with nothing spilling over to the next. While few women would approach life this way, this masculine trait does serve men well in times of intense growth or crisis.

The following qualities not only describe men but also reflect the deeper needs the soul virgin man hopes the women in his life will admire and encourage.

Significant

We've never met a man who could get enough affirmation, admiration, and respect, such as, "King Kong's got nothin' on you" (as he removes a large rock from the campsite) or "What a gentleman" (as he safely escorts a group of women from a concert to their cars). Men crave success, and their zeal for accomplishment demonstrates this. Women, take a closer look before blowing this off as an immature, overinflated "ego." A *man who feels significant will be more motivated to give respect and provide initiative.*

Now, granted, the masculine concept of "bigger is better" can be quite amusing. A recent lecture I attended on the genders stated the male brain is typically bigger than the female brain. However, the female brain is typically better connected between the right and left hemispheres and is more in tune with feelings. After the lecture, I remember thinking, *Theirs may work better, but who cares . . . mine's bigger!*

Strong

Men's greater muscle mass and size help them in being protectors and knights for their princesses. But male initiative in taking on challenges goes beyond the physical to deeper soul issues. Men love to be counted on and validated as a fortress of strength, both internal and external.

Stability in the midst of danger is part of this sought-after masculine strength. Winning battles and keeping one's word create self-esteem in men. Maintaining honor (that sometimes seems silly to women) is a part of God's image in the masculine. The chivalrous knight in shining armor who arrives just in the nick of time to protect and defend is a common feminine fantasy adapted from these masculine aspects of honor and strength.

Safe

Men desire a castle where they can retreat to relax, regroup, lick their wounds, and enjoy recreation. After slaying a couple dragons, their castle creates safety and comfort. Men see the world as a challenging competition, so the nurturing safety of something to eat and a little distraction is rather inviting. Then, all of a sudden, into this poor guy's comfortable fortress glides the princess, desiring to resolve issues and enjoy connecting conversation!

Simple

"My fiancé is so simple. He's all exhausted from helping move my things into my new apartment and ready to quit. Then I'll tell him what a great job he's doing and how I could never have accomplished it without him. All at once, he's ready for another two hours. I'm never that easy." Men do seem less complex and not as muddled with feelings. They are quite motivated by admiration and praise and more focused on the task at hand. Brain research shows that men tend to be more left-brained and analytical, with less connectivity to the creative right brain. This may be part of their hyper-focus and lack of multitasking. Like Sergeant Friday of *Dragnet*, they declare, "Just the facts, ma'am," as they bottom-line and compartmentalize things.

The Virtuous Man: Humble

Women sometimes wonder why men have a tendency to be arrogant, preoccupied, defensive, and self-centered. These are simply insecure distortions of the God-designed strengths of masculinity—a strong, proactive confidence and an ability to focus on the project at hand. A real man securely and non-defensively rests in his personal strengths. He knows who he is and has nothing to prove. This is where true humility begins, being confident in all God made him to be. Such confidence allows a man to forget about himself and simply enjoy others. With godly self-esteem, he can encourage the feminine roles without being defensive and even follow her intuitive lead at times in the dance of intimacy.

This humble confidence encourages the Christlike behavior of serving. Like his Master, a real man is strong enough to wash feet and become the force behind others' blossoming. He doesn't fear being upstaged by female beauty and power but celebrates it. The ballerina steals the show, and he is able to follow her cue while giving initiative and strength to the lifts and compelling dance movements. The virtuous, humble man exudes confidence, unselfishness, and proactivity. He is God's positive initiator through his service that is tailored to her needs. In turn, the virtuous woman affirms such men in their strength and humble self-confidence.

The Masculine Vocation in Intimacy: Humble Warrior Prince

John Eldredge writes, "Little boys yearn to know they are powerful, they are dangerous, they are someone to be reckoned with. . . . Like it or not, there is something fierce in the heart of every man."[1] A "humble warrior prince" describes the male's relational role. The masculine virtue of true and confident *humility* demonstrates the way men can assertively thrive, bringing out the best in themselves and others. A *warrior* passionately takes on challenges. Prince Charming and other *princes* of folklore initiate the movement into creating romantic fulfillment. Jesus, our warrior king and humble servant, creates the ultimate example for men to follow.

Warrior and Initiator

Men bring a different spin to intimacy than women with their need for adventurous challenge and competency. This warrior heart tackles new ventures but can sometimes get preoccupied with the task at hand, becoming defensive or withdrawing when he fears failure. He courageously risks rejection in pursuit of love but craves the alluring feminine response. The masculine soul longs for adventure. Unfortunately, a motivating factor behind male sexual addiction is an errant need for adventure as an antidote to boredom. Initiative and proactivity are important male qualities, which single women often lament they see so little of these days.

Strong Fortress

Men's strength in relationships is more than "slaying dragons"; it's an inner steadiness and ability to protect the women in his life. In some ways, this is a reflection of God himself: "The Lord is my rock, my fortress and my deliverer; my God is my rock, in whom I take refuge. He is my shield and the horn of my salvation, my stronghold" (Psalm 18:2). As a rock of strength, a man has in his soul a "provider syndrome" to care for the women God puts into his world.

Emotionally Even

A "sensitive rock" is what God calls the male to be as he empathetically listens to female feelings but then does not mirror them. Oh, the blessing and the curse of having a narrower range of feelings and the capacity to more easily contain them! With this emotional evenness comes the challenge of being self-disclosing and self-aware of the broad range of his emotions. If you're a male reader, the women in your life will become lonely and feel excluded if you don't develop such skills.

Bonding through Activity

How great would it be to draw close to the women in your life through Monday Night Football or PlayStation games? Yeah, right! For the most part, men bond more through activity. Though men have the capacity for conversation, it's not the default way of relating for most. Sports, projects, walks, and other forms of recreation can help men create a context to practice other intimacy skills, such as verbal conversation.

Spiritually Proactive

Women often state they desire a spiritual leader in the man they marry. Men aren't always sure what that "dude" looks like. One young couple being coached on their upcoming marriage tackled this issue. He knew she wanted a spiritual leader, but he was a relatively new Christian; she had grown up in the church. In frustration, he finally confessed, "You want me to get us a devotional book to read together. I've never been in a Christian bookstore and have no idea what you want. If you go get the book, I'll make sure we make the time to read it together." Alternatively, he might also have asked his pastor for coaching on the issue. With patient resolve, be willing as a couple to seek compromises "outside the box" as you work through fulfilling God's desire for masculine initiative in spiritual leadership.

Sexually Assertive

Men have more testosterone, the primary hormone for sexual desire. They tune in visually to the allure of specific physical attributes and respond more immediately to the sexual stimulation of their senses. In the dance of intimacy, men are often more assertive in their desire. They will be more likely to think erotic thoughts and seek to meet intimacy needs through initiating erotic behaviors.

Men and Women: Celebrating Differences

We would like to conclude with a brief look at some of the commonly perceived "incompatibilities" of *men* trying to relate with *women*. Here are but a few:

Focused on the task at hand (which is often some personal priority of his): Men have a knack for focusing on the task at hand based upon an internalized priority grid. It's fascinating how often things important to them seldom match up with their female counterparts. Such focus obviously has as much positive potential (as in fixing something that's broken) as it does negative (as in being so engrossed in a ballgame as to ignore the rest of civilization). Women, this is such a universal trait in men. May we make a suggestion? You can either think it's cute and *accommodate for it* or remain forever frustrated.

Bottom-line communication and asking questions for answers: Men aren't usually interested in what they describe as idle chitchat. "Don't tell me the whole story" and "Cut to the chase" are male mantras. They ask questions designed to solicit simple factual answers. This is quite unlike their female friends, who ask questions as a means of connecting through story. "Do you want to invite your roommate to come to the party?"—"Yes" or "No." Ladies, consider giving him the bottom line first. This can sometimes motivate him to listen to the rest of the story.

The provider syndrome (and its related idiosyncrasies): Men desire to provide. However, once they think they've fulfilled that role, the task is over, and it's time to kick back. "I grilled the steaks. What do you mean, 'help clean up'?" Sometimes too great a distinction exists between what's considered women's work versus men's work: "I moved the couch; can you bring me a cold one while you finish cooking dinner?" Guys, beware: women usually won't let you be this selfish.

Laid back and going with the flow: For the woman who's looking for initiative, a man can sometimes prove quite frustrating: "If it made a difference, I would have told you. I can

96

eat Chinese *or* Italian." Men often have a more laid-back approach to life unless a true priority is involved. Avoiding conflict and doing what's easier comes more naturally. Women, here's a suggestion: take a man at his word. Believe it or not, most of the time he really *doesn't* care. If after the fact you find he really did, that's a great opportunity to have a conversation about the importance of honest dialogue in relationships.

Remember, we're painting with a broad brush in describing masculinity and femininity. These are merely generalities, and not every description will fit every person. God designed each of us to embody a unique mix of masculine and feminine traits. In general, men will have a greater "mix" of masculine than feminine traits, and vice versa for women. Even still, understanding the uniqueness of each gender can be tremendously beneficial to successful relating with the opposite sex.

Now that we have a better understanding of the masculine, let's take a closer look at the other half of God's sexual metaphor: soul-sexy femininity.

Eight

Soul-Sexy Femininity

with Erica S. N. Tan and Anna Maya

Principle:

**God calls women to gracious responsiveness
and inner beauty**

Women call it mysterious. Men call it *confusing*! What a fascinating complexity the female gender is to men. We're not sure God ever really intended a total comprehension of women by men—their complexity is part of their mystery. However, men do need a basic understanding of the female psyche to enrich their intimate relationships with them.

How curious that men who love to master techno gadgets often view the female psyche with the same complication of the control panel on a commercial jetliner: "Okay, she's in a bad mood. Let's see, I think if I adjust these controls, turn these four switches off and these three on—or is it the other way around?" Men are typically much simpler. If they're in a bad mood, a hearty meal and admiration for a job well done can do wonders!

Men can benefit greatly from a basic understanding of the female psyche to enrich their intimate friendships. It isn't as impossible as it might seem. The soul-sexy woman desires to be valued and inspired—to be called out and pursued as a captivating beauty in her meaningful relationships with men.

Sabotaging Soul-Sexy Femininity

Worldly pressures seek to deny women's God-given femininity, preventing them from fully celebrating their own sexuality. Wonderful differences set them apart from men. Poor definitions, unfair comparisons, and cultural distortions often block women from embracing God's creative gift to them.

Poor Definitions and Stereotypes

So often we look for gender models in all the wrong places. An example of a poor definition is the range of culturally stereotyped women, often "celebrities," who are touted as standards for femininity. Facets of God's image of femininity exist in each, but fallible human icons will always fall short in providing a model of wholeness. God and Scripture alone are to be our standard of conduct and character.

Although women desire to be admired for their external beauty, soul-sexiness extends beyond their physical attributes. The media reinforces the stereotype that external appearance and a sexy body trump inner beauty and a woman's internal character. Women in Western societies dress to emphasize the body, sometimes leaving little to the imagination. This makes paying attention to a woman's soul-sexiness extremely difficult for men. Guys, women appreciate men who focus *on their person* and not just on the size and shape of their bodies. But women, let's face it: many men take their cues on how to treat you from the clothing (or how little of it) you choose to wear. They will often mirror the values you portray and value you no more than you value yourself.

Comparisons and Cultural Confusion

Women have the terrible habit of comparing themselves with other women. This diminishes their unique identity and self-worth as well as that of others. The comparisons women draw create a rather constricted view of what it means to be feminine. For example, if a woman upholds motherhood as *the* standard of femininity, she may not accept opportunities to develop other parts of herself apart from motherhood. She may have difficulty embracing the truth of who she's been created to be as a godly woman. This may also apply to her body image.

Runway models who often are five foot nine and 115 pounds rather than the more typical five foot five and 140-plus pounds lead to even more distorted perceptions and comparisons.

Women experience an internal tug-of-war between the secular world and the Church. The world communicates impossible messages about femininity that combine a "Barbie" sexiness with a "successful woman who plays like the boys" in the corporate arena. Meanwhile, the Church sometimes leans too heavily to the other extreme, overly emphasizing a femininity that should be expressed through service-oriented roles, such as wife, mother, teacher, and nursery worker. Somewhere between these exhausting messages, godly soul-sexiness gets lost. Men need to better understand how to relate to feminine sexuality in ways that honor both women and God. Women need not only to understand but also to *embrace* their multifaceted uniqueness.

An Armoire—Traits of Femininity

If men favor chests of drawers, women most closely resemble armoires. Throw open the doors of an armoire and everything is visible. It has no compartments, and everything is openly interactive—shelves of shoe boxes, sweaters, and underwear. Yet everything has a secure place to rest.

As you think through the following qualities of women, remember that they both describe femininity and are common female needs. Men exemplify the needs for significance, strength, safety, and simplicity. Women have the following qualities, which they hope to have affirmed by the men in their lives: being special, sensitive, secure, and surprising.

Special

A woman desires others to value her as special—that is, distinctive and extraordinary. In the same way men respond to admiration and respect, women flourish with heartfelt compliments, knowing they have a unique appeal. "I am the rose of Sharon, the lily of the valley" (Song of Songs 2:1 NLT). The beloved (the woman in the story) is saying this to her lover. Roses grow singularly, unique and separate from other flowers. In response, her lover declares, "Yes, compared to other women, my beloved is like a lily among thorns" (v. 2 NLT). The beloved pronounces her uniqueness, and her lover affirms her as such. Every man should learn to give sincere affirmation to the women in his life—but especially to the one who is his potential Eve.

Sensitive

Women often have an intuitive feel for relationships. They possess a sensitive and sympathetic ability to respond to the feelings and needs of others. Their empathic responsiveness reflects the integration of their awareness of people, situations, thoughts, and emotions—much like items in an armoire. Therefore, women have the ability to quickly size up a situation, the people involved, and their possible thoughts and emotions.

As previously stated, research supports that a woman's brain and her emotions are better connected. The tendency for women to multitask is facilitated by the greater connectivity between the creative side of the right brain with the more analytical side of the left. This enables most women to attend to more than one thing at a time. They can listen to the television, keep an eye on the party, and have a coherent conversation—all at the same time.

Secure

Women are typically quite in tune with the safety needs of those around them. Married and single women alike make comments such as, "Fasten your seatbelt" or "You're tired, get some rest." My (Erica's) mother has a radar that detects hidden dangers surrounding her family. When her "alarm" goes off, she unleashes a litany of warnings about potential endangerment (for example, "Don't go surfing because it might be unsafe today"). As with Jesus, who likened himself to a protective mother hen, women desire to keep their loved ones safe. Guys sometimes complain that their girlfriends nag a lot. However, many times it's about one or two items regarding personal safety that haven't been adequately attended to by the male. While women have the ability to recognize and nurture the needs of others, they also desire to feel safe and protected in relationship with a man who is dependable.

Surprising

A comment men often make about women concerns how unpredictable they are. Feminine needs and responses remain elaborate and complex. Yet paradoxically, this trait also supplies the mysterious adventure men enjoy. A humorous example is a woman's tendency to pack for every occasion in one suitcase—to dress up or down, for warm or cold, and for rain or shine. Women call it "remaining flexible," often leaving their male counterparts bewildered: how can a five-day trip possibly require five pairs of pants, three skirts, three sweaters, six shirts, two dresses, and five pairs of shoes? Compared to the straightforwardness of men, women are indeed entertainingly complex.

The Virtuous Woman: Modest

According to Webster's dictionary, modesty is defined as "freedom from conceit or vanity" and "propriety in dress, speech, or conduct."[1] An example of such modesty is Jesus's mother, Mary. In response to discovering her pregnancy (which seemed for obvious reasons an impossibility), Mary's acceptance of the angel's news about her miraculous conception was simple and full of humility: "I am the Lord's servant" (Luke 1:38).

God made Eve with a modesty that protected her power and beauty. Her allure was not for her own gain but rather to empower her in motivating the best in Adam, her companion. This lack of vanity and her sense of what was proper gave her a mysterious appeal. She would reveal her complete self at the proper time in the loving safety of committed relationship.

Does this mean modesty clashes with being soul-sexy and alluring? Author Wendy Shallit says sexual modesty might squelch a *superficial* type of allure, but that's the stuff one-night stands are made of. The *true* feminine allure (which modesty protects and inspires) doesn't squelch a woman's sexuality. As Shallit writes, "In fact, it is more likely to enkindle it."[2] "Letting it all hang out" leaves little to the imagination, undermining the thrill that should accompany the gentle unfolding of feminine mystery.

Deep within the soul of a man lies honor—a desire to pursue, win, and provide for his woman. With a soul-sexy allure tempered by modesty, women elicit from their men patient respect, loving attention, and complete commitment. Women need to understand and practice a healthy privacy and self-directed modesty in enjoying the benefits of their sexual beauty without manipulation or pretense. Done rightly, this encourages the men in their lives to be honorable and respectful in their relationships with them. It also helps to prevent either from reducing their relationship to selfishly chasing erotic adventures.

The Feminine Vocation in Intimacy: Soulfully Powerful Beauty

"Can there be any doubt that Eve is the crown of creation? Not an afterthought. Not a nice addition like an ornament on a tree. She is God's final touch, his *pièce de résistance*. She fills a place in the world nothing and no one else can fill."[3] Before I (Erica) read this quote from John and Stasi Eldredge's book *Captivating*, I genuinely struggled with the idea that divine beauty is fashioned in all women. The pervasiveness of physical attraction as a standard for beauty was something I felt I couldn't live up to because my physical attributes seemed diametrically opposed to those exemplified by supermodels. They're tall; I'm short. They've got long, flowing hair; mine is short and spiky. They have big, beautiful eyes; fatigue makes my almond-shaped Asian eyes resemble slits. However, the pronouncement of Eve's status as the "crown of creation" gives me hope—beauty *is* inherent in me, in other women, in *all* women.

Beautiful and Powerful

Women help men seek deeper levels of soulful intimacy through their soul-sexy femininity. Women aren't reluctant to experience the power of their emotions. God gave women allure that draws men into achieving levels of emotional intimacy they might otherwise struggle to reach on their own. Women use body language and nonverbal communication to convey deep messages without uttering a single word. That "wink" or special look can make a man's heart jump, propelling him into soulful connecting.

104

Within intimate gender relationships, the female beauty and power can also become distorted. For example, some women learn early in life to wield sexual power to manipulate men. Rather than bringing out the best in men, they attempt to control them with their erotic sexuality.

Maternally Nurturing

Nurturing comes naturally in relational settings for both married and single women. Maternal nurturing can be seen in a woman's interactions with those around her. For example, one of my (Erica's) friends just established a cell phone plan for her parents so they would have phone access during their move to Europe. She is very much in tune with the needs of others. Such maternal nurturing goes beyond a desire for having children to a deeper ability for fostering and preserving life. Even the way God chose to create life illustrates this. Men initiate by *providing* the seed, but women *nurture* the seed through their bodies to fertilization and then *preserve* life through birth and beyond. And this desire to nurture isn't just found in women who like children. When soul-sexy women are grounded in their God-given identities, they elicit the best from others with whom they are in relationship.

Emotionally Variable

Women are full of surprises emotionally. Some of this can be attributed to hormones, particularly during certain times of the month. However, emotional variability is much bigger than mere hormonal fluctuations. Women experience and take pleasure in a wider range of emotions than most men. Their brains tune in to feelings better. This benefits a woman's relationships by enabling her to bond more holistically. Unfortunately, it sometimes also serves to override her ability at logical, linear thought.

This explains why many women follow their hearts when it comes to relationships. Her friend might ask, "Why are you dating him?" Because she's so emotionally connected, she might not be able to see her girlfriend's point of view that he's obviously using her. This emphasizes a woman's need for female friends in her life to give her greater objectivity when her emotions might be clouding her own good judgment.

Socially Connected

While men see life as a competitive arena, women see life more as a community of people who deeply connect. Intimate relationships help women find identity and a deeper meaning to life. Men also prioritize connecting relationships; however, theirs look quite different. I (Anna) remember when a professor shared with our class about a time her husband ran into an old friend at the airport. The two guys quickly pulled out their electronic organizers, updated each other on their plans for the future, and were quickly on their way. Afterward he commented, "It was so good to see him." She replied, "See him? You barely looked up at him!" Women have a gift for achieving deep degrees of social and emotional intimacy. Perhaps this is why women enjoy hour-long phone conversations and knowing the *details* of their friends' lives that men generally find cumbersome and unnecessary.

Soulfully Spiritual

Like the armoire, the woman's soul will be less likely to "compartmentalize" their faith and values. The high population of women in churches demonstrates their deep, spiritual desire to commune with others and with God.

Christian women long for men who can model, encourage, and initiate a strong faith in their relationship. God is the one who breaks the power of evil in the human heart and creates trustworthiness and stability, qualities dear to the feminine soul. Women appreciate men who bring such stability and trust to the relationship, especially when it comes to faith and values. Soulful spirituality is characterized by wisdom and virtue. Scripture calls women back to the spiritual importance of their "inner self, the unfading beauty of a gentle and quiet spirit, which is of great worth in God's sight" (1 Peter 3:4).

Sexually Responsive

Women have libido and enjoy erotic sexuality, yet what turns them on is likely different from what turns on their male counterparts. You might have heard the old adage, "women give sex for love, and men give love for sex." In its sinfully broken form, this statement rings true. Some women do give of their erotic sexuality to get what they *believe* is love. But even in healthy relationships, women who experience emotional intimacy *are* more likely to respond erotically to their partners. Women typically don't think as much about erotic sexuality as men, except in Coupling or in the early years of marriage due to the excitement of new romance and heightened sensuality. However, she can revel in her allure and often may become excited by her man's initiative toward her and respond, "I hadn't thought of that tonight, but now that you mention it . . ."

Women and Men: Celebrating Differences

As in chapter 7, here is now a brief look at some of the commonly perceived "incompatibilities" of *women* trying to relate with *men*:

Unpredictability: Women keep men on their toes. Men need to embrace these seemingly illogical shifts and whimsical nature. For example, the writing team for this book (consisting of men and women) was out for dinner one night. The men thought it fascinating when the waiter asked Anna what vegetable she wanted and she replied, "Why don't you surprise me?" That's certainly not a typical *male* response!

Connection through questions and conversations: What women call "connecting conversation" with their girlfriends, men call "idle chitchat." When women ask men questions, a man can feel interrogated and think, *I've got to fix it*, rather than sensing her desire to simply connect. "How was your day?" is rich with possibility for connecting conversation, until the typical male responses of "Fine" or "Why are you asking?" If you're a guy and this is your typical response, ask the women in your life for suggested responses that might help you open the doorway to deeper connecting with them.

Maternal instinct to protect and nurture: One young husband wondered what had happened to his girlfriend when she became his wife. With phrases like "We need to write wills" and "Look where you're going," she had transformed from laid back into a woman on a mission. In talking with other husbands, he discovered many wives have a mother hen nature as they cared for their "nest." He didn't complain, though—his wife's had saved him from several possible car accidents!

Different values and priorities: One woman commented to me that her favorite Christmas gift from her boyfriend was a used book. Knowing that she'd also received expensive jewelry, this seemed surprising to me. She explained the book took much thoughtfulness to locate. That "scored more points" than the jewelry because it showed he was thinking about her unique personality. To her, he was demonstrating he valued their relationship by investing significant time and energy on her behalf.

We hope you now have a better appreciation for the fascinating differences God wove into the very fabric of the genders. Often the differences that drive us crazy are the same characteristics that draw us toward one another like a moth to the flame. But how do we allow ourselves to enjoy the magnetic attraction of the opposite sex without getting burned in the process? More importantly, what do we do when we discover the flame we're drawn to isn't on the outside, but is instead a sexual burning deep inside our very souls?

Nine

So ... What Do I Do with My Sexual Surging?

Principle:

God has a purpose for sexual desire in the single adult

How do you react to the word *horny*? We received many different comments, from "I hate that word" to "No other word expresses the strong way my sex drive sometimes seems to run my life." We asked for synonyms and received, among others: frisky, randy, amorous, charged, hot, aroused, turned on, hormonal. We ultimately decided not to use it—thinking it emphasized too many unhealthy stereotypes. Instead, we prefer to use words that better define the complex concept of sexual desire and the underlying longing for genuine intimacy.

Defining Sexual Desire

God created humans with a rich sexual desire that should motivate us toward intimacy. "Horny," "randy," or "hot" simplistically reduce sexual desire to a one-dimensional hormonal thing we must either indulge or alleviate. Healthy sexual desire needs to reflect all three dimensions of body, soul, and spirit.

God created our *bodies* with a complex hormonal makeup that creates desire through testosterone and other body chemistry in both men and women. Our bodies at times surge with sexual arousal. One female stated it well: "Certain days of the month, I'm so turned on I whistle back at construction workers!" These sexual desires can get us into trouble if we don't understand their purpose or if we try to repress them.

Our *soul* (with our mind, emotions, and ability to make deliberate choices) adds complexity to the physical aspect of sexual desire. We aren't simply "in heat" like the family pet. We can choose either to feed our arousal or to discipline it with healthy fantasy and relational interaction. With the *spiritual* part of us longing for intimacy and completion, we can reach out to create intimate relationship with our Creator. God also gave us a tangible way to connect with this divine reality, allowing humans to find deep fulfillment through mating for a lifetime with an opposite-sex partner in marriage. Thus, our sexual desire can drive us toward long-term godly relationships.

Two concepts well describe this three-dimensional surging of sexual desire. First is the concept of energy or electricity. Sexual *surges* and *surging* portray more accurately the sexual electricity God put inside us—charged and energized. Like the Energizer Bunny, we are powered by our sexual current into all sorts of behaviors and intimate relationships. "Surge protectors" (godly boundaries) must also be put into place to discipline this energy in our connecting and coupling relationships. For example, certain levels of surging may indicate for some a need to hang out with same-sex friends rather than attend a singles mixer and run the risk of inappropriate behavior with the opposite sex.

A second concept stems from the Italian word *amore*. Our English word *amorous* implies someone feeling turned on not by mere hormones but rather a desire to sexually relate, motivated by a hunger for intimacy and connection. The Elvis song "Burning Love" is one of a myriad of songs popularizing such a longing, burning with desire.

Instead, we prefer to describe this sexual longing as an *ache*. Every person experiences this love ache at times—an intense sexual craving or yearning that goes much deeper than simplistic horniness.

Intimacy Needs and the Sexual Ache

The term *sexual ache* reminds us that our sexual surges aren't just about hormones and engaging in sexual activity. It's also about trying to fill a deep longing inside us. We aren't ignoring the fact that erotic sexual behaviors create excitement.

However, we can trivialize our sexual desire by merely chasing after a buzz. Whether we're consciously aware of it or not, the yearning for intimacy is always pushing us from within. Some become so desperate to silence it that they turn to all forms of compulsions or addictions: drugs, alcohol, work, partying, addictive hobbies, "serial" relationships, or a string of one-night stands.

In reality, the fundamental nature of this ache stems from a desire to be vulnerable and intimately known by another, revealing who we are at our deepest level of existence. It's a yearning to be unconditionally accepted, without mask or facade. Marital sexual intercourse was designed by God to be the ultimate expression of such "naked and unashamed" vulnerability and intimacy. In fact, Hebrew Scripture uses the word *yada* (to know) as a word for sexual intimacy: "Adam *knew* his wife Eve, and she conceived" (Genesis 4:1 NKJV, emphasis added). The essence of desire becomes an intimate "knowing" deep within the heart.

God created us with the capacity for such intimacy of the soul. But two critical points must be emphasized about this deep level of intimacy. First, only God, through our relationship with Christ, can ever completely satisfy our intimacy needs for being unconditionally known and accepted. The intimate lovemaking between a man and a woman (as good and complete as that may feel) is only a taste of our ultimate love relationship with God. *Being truly known can only be experienced in a pure, intimate, unadulterated experience between an individual and God himself.*

Second, the human intimacy God intended to salve the ache can only be experienced through soul virginity within the safe commitment of covenant companionship (marriage). Although Hollywood would argue otherwise, casual sex and indulging the rush of erotic lust will *never* adequately scratch the itch or create an intimacy that completely satisfies.

So what should you do with this ache as a single adult? Take a lot of cold showers, settle for false intimacy, or masturbate a lot? Not hardly. *We must discover the purpose for the ache and understand why such deep longing exists*—and what to do when it comes to the surface—if we are ever to be all God created us to be as soul virgins.

Distorting versus Accepting Sexual Surges (the Ache)

We live in an oversexualized culture—one that is absolutely obsessed and saturated with sexual thoughts and images. One option for dealing with the ache would be to indulge every sexual surge, ignoring soul virginity altogether. "What if God doesn't meet my 'needs'?" "What if the rapture happens before I've had sex?" "What if I want to have fun with that hot little thing who says she loves me?" You might simply reject God's plan because the culture does in its obsession with genital sexuality. Besides, you've never been taught to think through it any differently, anyway.

Jesus was famished after forty days of fasting in the wilderness (see Matthew 4:1–11). Satan came and suggested he might make bread out of some stones lying around. Jesus refused this picnic as he waited for the angels who would later bring him a heavenly feast. Has Satan been deceiving you into making pitiful picnics to deal with your sexual ache?

The Church, seeing the distortion in our culture, has traditionally responded with what initially appears as godly wisdom: "Sex is for marriage—be abstinent." But this statement *without any practical explanation of what is meant* by itself can send a disturbing underlying message: "We aren't comfortable discussing what to do with your sexual desires as a single person. If you just abstain from all erotic sexual behaviors, you'll forget you're a sexual being and won't struggle anymore." Another unspoken message then becomes, "As a single person you are asexual until marriage—then you can turn your sexual switch 'on.'" Obviously, single adults *are* sexual beings and *do* have sexual desires. It seems the Church sometimes views the eternal Creator as throwing up his hands in shock: "Oh no, single adults have sexual feelings and desire, and now they aren't getting married until almost thirty! This sure has caught me off guard. What will I do?" That's ridiculous! God knew exactly what he was doing.

A special note for men: you might sometimes feel God gave you way more sexual "burn" than was necessary when it seems half the desire would have gotten the job done. Yet, the Creator uses this seeming "oversexed-ness" to drive men to draw closer to him, to *connect* with female and male friends, and to initiate meaningful coupling relationships—all of which are great antidotes to lust. Gentle waves of female estrogen would not likely have broken down the male focus on work or play to make a guy pursue intimate relationships. This wouldn't have driven him to his knees before God, seeking help to find discipline for this tidal wave.

So then why was this sexual ache given to you even as a single adult? Why wasn't the switch left "off" by God until your wedding night? Here's the honest truth you must accept: your sexual ache was purposefully designed by God to motivate you (body, soul, and spirit) toward an intimate connection with God, an intimate connection with other members of the body of Christ, and eventually an intimate connection with a future spouse. Even if you never marry, the sexual ache is the divinely created vehicle God uses to give you a longing for intimate connection with himself and with others.

Appreciating and Disciplining Sexual Surges

Inside every single adult, the sexual ache burns. But how is it that many single adults thrive while others either wither away in loneliness and resentment or hedonistically indulge sexual buzzes? Joyful soul virgins experience intense sexual surging and long for their Adam or Eve, too. So what's the difference? Here are a few of the ideas that I (Michael Todd) and other single adults have found helpful to live in contentment and work through our own sexual surging.

Keep in mind that none of us even come close to perfection when it comes to always putting these skills into consistent practical application. God is still in the process of teaching me the very things we're advocating in this book. Nonetheless, this still remains our standard for practice as soul virgins. Yet, we can take comfort in the fact that the apostle Paul must have felt much the same when he confessed, "Not that I have already obtained all this, or have already been made perfect, but I press on to take hold of that for which Christ Jesus took hold of me. Brothers, I do not consider myself yet to have taken hold of it. But one thing I do: Forgetting what is behind and straining toward what is ahead, I press on toward the goal to win the prize for which God has called me heavenward in Christ Jesus" (Philippians 3:12–14). Also, a personal acquaintance with God's ER has at times provided much needed healing and insight.

Understanding Love and Eros

In Greek literature, many words were used for "love." Three prominent words used to describe love were *eros*, *phileo*, and *agape*. These represented different expressions of sexuality. As the root for our English word *erotic*, *eros* embodies a passionate type of love for another person that creates erotic sexual connection. Eros gives us the picture of an exciting magnetic field with bodies and minds attracting and resonating with sensual delight. *Phileo* is commonly known as "brotherly love"—that is, the friendly warmth and authentic connection you might experience with a close friend. *Agape* represents the intentional and unconditional love God has for us—given with no strings attached and without demanding anything in return.

For the Christian desiring to live by God's economy, eros is something primarily intended for the marital relationship. Erotic *attraction* permeates even connecting relationships but should be disciplined and expressed in a mature and limited manner. Our godless society knows little about the commitment of agape or the authenticity of phileo. Consequently, it is obsessed with eros. In fact, *our culture would have us believe eros is the only legitimate form of love and sexual expression.*

The Art of Redirecting and Reframing Sexual Desire

So what are we supposed to do with this sexual ache as a Christian? The first step is to reject the culture's lie that love and sexual expression can be found only in erotic love. Two practical tools that can help manage sexual surges are redirecting and reframing. *Redirecting* takes sexual energy and uses it to motivate other activities and accomplishments. *Reframing* sees into the deeper meaning of sexual desire, allowing such perspective to inspire greater wholeness.

Redirecting eros into phileo and agape love can make a big difference. What does this mean practically? When your sexual ache is strongest, your greatest need as a follower of Christ is to actively seek a meaningful connection with God and with your brothers and sisters in Christ. Recall that your deepest need isn't for a sexual buzz but rather for genuine intimacy. To meet your intimacy needs in healthy and godly ways may mean taking time out to: experience personal worship time with God through prayer, listen to praise music, read or study Scripture, talk with a friend by phone, socialize with a church group, or spend the evening with a close friend over dinner engaging in meaningful, "below the surface" conversation.

Honest and intimate same-sex friendships with accountability (and sometimes even commiseration!) can help absorb sexual energy in healthy ways. You can redirect it into other activities as well. Strenuous physical activity increases adrenaline and can help you cope. Get a punching bag or join a kickboxing class. Learn to dance and do it with enthusiasm. Hiking, working out, and vigorous exercise can help redirect sexual energy. I remember how I (Doug) was helped after my divorce by running the 10K Peachtree Road Race and enjoying a country dancing class.

Reframing creatively renews your mind sexually, allowing you to seek new definitions and perspectives for old ideas. It's like putting a new frame on a favorite picture, helping you draw out things from the painting you've never seen before but that have always been there. Reframe your sexual surges from simple hormonal horniness, focusing instead on your deeper desire for intimacy. With this reframe, physical affection (pats and hugs) and appropriate nurturing touch can meet some of these deeper needs. Enjoy the freedom of being single and engaging in authentic relationship with friends and family. Reframe the idea that enjoying companionship with the opposite sex *has* to include erotic sexual behaviors.

Put a bigger frame around your sexual energy, one that allows your ache to motivate you toward compassion, depth of character, and adventures in true intimacy. Be courageous and forward-thinking as you integrate the valuable concepts of soul virginity. Though this time of single sexual challenge is neither fun nor easy, it can be seen as powerful training for learning critical relational skills and for shaping your character. Sexual temptations will confront you even in marriage. Erotic sexual fulfillment isn't a "right" but a blessing that God gives, one that should be enjoyed only in a God-honoring manner and context. Reframing this issue in coupling relationships is an opportunity to learn lessons about self-control and unselfish nurturing important to future Covenanting.

I remember a young man who came to me whining that his wife was having a terrible pregnancy and they hadn't made love for three months. I replied, "Were you never single? Sex isn't a right; it's a privilege. Nothing is going to explode or fall off. Practice other types of intimacy and reach out beyond yourself to nurture your wife in this time of temporary celibacy." My fear is that he'd never practiced soul virginity or incorporated soul virgin disciplines. Learning to reframe and see the big picture as a single person is great preparation for healthy future relationships, including marriage.

The Ineffectiveness of "White-Knuckling": Embracing Your Sexual Surges

Sometimes single adults are encouraged to fight sexual surges. Though not technically incorrect, such advice can lead you into an ineffective pattern the Twelve Step recovery community calls "white-knuckling." Sexaholics Anonymous uses the term to refer to sex addicts who've stopped inappropriate sexual activities in their external behaviors but *have not given up the underlying lust in their hearts.* They are attempting to stop inappropriate behaviors through sheer willpower alone, without the power of a transformed heart.

The word picture of white-knuckling is that of a sex addict tightly clutching the arms of a chair while staring at the *Sports Illustrated* swimsuit special on TV, saying to himself, "I'm not going to get aroused, I'm not going to act out. . . ." With this as his only weapon, failure is sure to follow. Remember our inside-out model (chapter 3). This person's heart hasn't come to the place of trusting God and embracing his sexual economy. He is merely trying to govern external behaviors with no *internal* motivation to turn off the television.

If you choose to focus on dealing with the sexual ache by restraint alone (i.e., "I just need to focus on not thinking about sex until I get married"), you will find yourself obsessing about it 24/7! If you've ever tried this method, you know exactly what we're talking about. In actuality, this approach egocentrically places the focus back on you and ensures the only relationship that will grow is the one with yourself. Don't white-knuckle; redirect and reframe as you mature in deeper soul virgin attitudes.

The Ultimate Purpose of Desire: Enlarging Our Hearts

We never want to simplistically imply that dealing with the sexual ache comes easily for singles. Though you may practice these skills over a lifetime, the surging and aching will remain. However, you will expand your heart's capacity to love. Author Paula Rinehart encourages single adults so beautifully: "The pain of unmet desire can actually enlarge our hearts. The more we let ourselves long for life, though it brings the ache of incompleteness, the more we are actually able to savor the joys that come our way."[1]

To acknowledge your sexual surges, allowing them to push you toward healthy intimate relationships, is quite the adventure. No one else can do the tough but rewarding work for you. Each must "work out your own salvation [daily walk] with fear and trembling; for it is God who works in you both to will and to do for His good pleasure" (Philippians 2:12–13 NKJV). Soul virgin singles learn to master the skills for *going beyond their sexual longings to a larger capacity for love*—learning to give and to receive in relationships, building a supportive network of friends, and risking romantic coupling relationships.

Scripture gives strong encouragement that can be applied to your sexual ache: "Consider it a sheer gift, friends, when tests and challenges come at you from all sides. You know that under pressure, your faith-life is forced into the open and shows its true colors. So don't try to get out of anything prematurely. Let it do its work so you become mature and well-developed, not deficient in any way" (James 1:2–4 Message). Your sexual ache is indeed an indispensable part of your life by divine design, helping you grow up and connect more deeply with your Christian brothers and sisters. Choose to discipline and redirect your sexual surges. Then put on your dancing shoes—you won't want to sit this one out.

Ten

The Dance of Desire

Honoring Brothers and Sisters

Principle:
Seek to both enjoy and protect others sexually

I remember being a Christian single adult in the sexual confusion of the sixties and seventies, longing for some positive guidance for my sexual desires. You can imagine my heartfelt appreciation the day I came across this powerful story written by missionary Walter Trobisch:

> Once upon a time there was a tiger. He was captured and put in a cage. The keeper's task was to feed him and guard him.
>
> But the keeper wanted to make the tiger his friend. He always spoke to him in a friendly voice whenever he came to his cage. The tiger, however, always looked at him with hostility in his green, glowing eyes. He followed every movement of the keeper, ready to spring on him.
>
> The keeper was afraid of the tiger and asked God to tame him.
>
> One evening, when the keeper had already gone to bed, a little girl got lost in the vicinity of the tiger's cage and came too near to the iron bars. The tiger reached out with his claws. There was a blow, a scream. When the keeper arrived he found dismembered human flesh and blood.
>
> Then the keeper knew that God had not tamed the tiger. His fear grew. He drove the tiger into a dark hole where no one could come close to him. Now the tiger roared day and night. The terrible sound disturbed the keeper so that he could no longer sleep. It reminded him of his guilt. Always

in his dreams he saw the torn body of the little girl. Then he cried out in his misery. He prayed to God that the tiger might die.

God answered him, but the answer was different from what the keeper had expected. God said, "Let the tiger into your house, into the rooms where you live, even into your most beautiful room."

The keeper had no fear of death. He would rather die than go on hearing the roar of the tiger. So he obeyed. He opened the door of the cage and prayed, "Thy will be done."

The tiger came out and stood still. They looked into each other's eyes for a long time. As soon as the tiger noticed that the keeper had no fear and that he breathed quietly, he lay down at his feet . . .

After some years the two became good friends. The keeper could touch the tiger, even put his hand between his jaws. But he never dared to take his eyes off the tiger. When they looked at each other they recognized each other and were glad they belonged together and that each was necessary to the other.[1]

Sexual issues haven't changed much in the past forty years but have only grown more confusing. Keeping the tiger of your sexual desire under lock and key (and even driving it into the deep cave of sexual repression) only serves to intensify its menacing roar in your life. Only when you risk inviting it into the most beautiful rooms of your house—staring it in the eyes as you do—will you tame the tiger within.

We can embrace our sexual surges. However, we also must learn to protect and inspire one another as we choose to enter the sexual dance.

Desire and Two Types of Sexual Relating

In chapter 1 we described sexuality as God's grand demonstration of creative love. Two types of sexual relating flow out of this amazing creation: *gender* relating and *erotic* relating. How we enjoy and discipline each is unique.

Gender Relating

The family is God's central unit for gender sexual relating. Moms, dads, sisters, and brothers—all sexual beings with desires—build deeply loving relationships together. The language of this type of sexual relating might be called "social" or "friendly" (incorporating phileo and agape love) rather than erotic or romantic. Dads and other men help sons learn things that men do, including how to affirm and protect. Moms and other women teach daughters honor, modesty, and how to playfully react with feminine allure.

Even in healthy families, sexual surges still occur. A dad or brother may notice his daughter's or sister's feminine body or wiles, yet *godly boundaries are maintained.* Desires are not repressed but rather become the motivational energy to convert gender attraction into building meaningful connections with opposite-sex family members. This prepares them for future opposite-sex connecting relationships outside the family.

The nuclear family was intended to model God's family. Beginning with more general connecting friendships, Christian brothers and sisters move into satisfying gender relating that may eventually lead to Coupling—albeit with an *underlying tension of eros.* As romantic relationships blossom, the dance of desire takes on a more sensual, erotic flair.

Erotic Relating

In Coupling, sexual expression goes beyond family socializing toward erotic and romantic relating, as attraction is expressed personally and exclusively. Eros is appropriately engaged with 3-D body, soul, and spirit expressions of sexual attraction. Coupling relationships begin to enjoy erotic sexual behaviors within maturely and prayerfully applied limits. Yet the real focus remains on their desire for more intimately knowing one another. The unique ways God created men and women sexually for the dance of desire come into play.

Our hope is that each of you will step back from your own masculinity or femininity, seeking to more objectively understand the opposite-sex reality of your brothers or sisters in this dance of desire. If you're reading this chapter without occasionally commenting, "No way! I'm sure they don't really think or act like *that*," you probably aren't getting it. After all, men and women *are* very different in their sexual responses.

Men and the Sexual Dance

Too often men are sold short with comments like, "All he thinks about is sex," or "He's a man; he can't help being sexually aggressive." The truth is, men *can* desire emotional connection, be sensitive, and thrive on romantic interplay. Yet men need to realize the dance of intimacy will flow better if they orchestrate their own needs around the woman's needs and responses.

The human male can be as fascinating as the female sexually —not as complex, but equally interesting in his contribution to the dance. At the risk of stereotyping, the following demonstrates some of the ways most men differ from women in their sexual style.

Assertive

With more testosterone and the absence of menstrual fluctuation, men generally possess a more consistent and assertive sex drive. In conjunction with this hormonal push, men typically engage in sexual thoughts with greater frequency, which also heightens sexual desire. Men naturally enjoy initiating, whether in friendship, playful flirting, or erotic sexual behaviors. (Unfortunately, much of the broken masculinity in Western culture these days has been in this area, with men reverting in great numbers toward passivity. This has in part been driven by fear—often rooted in childhood trauma and a societal overreaction to male aggression.)

With a more assertive sexual desire, men will instigate erotic connection more frequently. Of course, men need to guard themselves so they pursue such behaviors only within Coupling —and true sex only within Covenanting (marriage). With godly discipline, this assertiveness can become a fun part of maleness in creating intimacy.

Sexually Connecting

The need for adventure and playfulness permeates true masculinity. Physical activity and recreation are ways men affirm one another. Men also experience affirmation from women through physical affection. Erotic connection can make a man feel like everything is okay. Physical touch can be a great way to make up after a fight (within the godly, mutually agreed-upon boundaries for a growing coupling relationship). However, men (single and married) can sometimes easily be tempted to turn to the erotic to satisfy even their *non-erotic* needs, such as their more general need for touch, affirmation, or even adventure. Girlfriends may notice their men seem more relationally connected after receiving physical affection. This isn't necessarily a bad thing: physical affection *does* tend to make a man feel affirmed like little else does.

| MEN : | *physical intimacy* | → | connects the soul | → | *leads to emotional closeness* |

Visual

Women notice men and create mental imagery. However, this differs dramatically from the male process. Men zoom in visually on female parts and curves. They are much more specific with their visual erotic cues and mental imagery—breasts, buttocks, navel, legs, and so on. Erotic arousal can happen very quickly.

Men may see a sexual cue in their environment and run with it. A woman may think, "My bra strap is showing; let me push it back." The man sees the red bra strap and wonders if the panties match. His fantasy is off and running unless he exercises integrity to rein in his mind. Female fantasy creates sensual pictures or focuses on the person, noticing things like smile, voice, and emotional response. Guys have to work harder at discipline because their images involve female body parts and behaviors—an entirely different reality.

Predictably Quick and Playful

Men are less complex than their female counterparts and more predictable in what arouses them erotically. With an "eternal adolescence" and a childlike curiosity, guys experience more immediate enjoyment of the sexual cues around them. They like what they see, wishing they could touch and explore. Men may get aroused quickly and sometimes neglect the emotional connecting women desire. They must learn to slow down, avoiding obsessive sexual behaviors and the objectification of women. This sexual integrity takes practice but rewards them with skills that will someday make them great husbands.

Women and the Sexual Dance

For all the positive improvements enjoyed by women, feminism and the sexual revolution of the 1960s and 1970s also, sadly, robbed women of part of their sexual soul. We wish we could say this phenomenon hasn't negatively affected the Christian singles' community, but it has. Christian women have increasingly been pressured to become aggressive sexually. In this *absence* of modesty and godly feminine intuition, women often make poor choices and get wounded by men they thought they could trust but who turn out to be unworthy of their trust after all.

Sitcoms such as *Seinfeld* and *Sex in the City* unrealistically portray women who are casual about erotic sexual involvement, never get too attached, care little about commitment, and keep emotions uninvolved so as to not get hurt. Further confusion arises when women are also asked to give romantic soul to their casual sexual activity by being a tender, receptive partner—even though their commitment and love needs in the relationship are being ignored. This pattern leaves women dissatisfied and broken, rather than joyfully responsive.

Receptive

Men often buy the myth that women have less interest in erotic sexuality. But women do have desire and enjoy such interaction. They simply approach it differently. Recent research shows women have a more "receptive" type of desire. Females don't think about erotic sexual interactions as much (especially after the thrill of a new relationship has quieted). Yet when approached by their men, they can often respond passionately. This receptivity is not passive but wonderfully modest as it acts *in response to male initiative*. Most women report thinking of sex less frequently than their male counterparts. For them, erotic involvement is more an emotional choice and less hormonally driven.

Emotionally Connecting

When the modern woman attempts to divorce erotic behaviors from loving tenderness and the feeling of being cherished, she loses who God created her to be. These latter qualities should never be abandoned by a woman. God gave her the wonderful ability to keep erotic expression soulfully intimate. Women bring so much of their soul to the dance.

Chantal's favorite memory with Tyson was a long walk on the beach—simply hanging out, talking, and holding hands by the salty air and surf. For her, kissing and caressing may follow the walk, which enables her to feel emotionally bonded. But Tyson's physical advances *before* the emotional connecting may seem pushy and intrusive to her.

Men and women have different entryways in approaching one another. Females should be careful not to become too emotionally driven, demand "perfect" conditions, or require the man to jump through multiple hoops to "prove" himself. She should also try to see his point of view that erotic connecting *can* be a legitimate way to make up after a fight.

WOMEN	:	emotional closeness	→	connects the heart	→	opens door to physical intimacy

Personal

Women's attractions and fantasies typically involve the whole person, not just body parts or the anticipation of a specific physical activity. Women notice character traits, tone of voice, communication styles, and the way personalities blend. My wife, Catherine, likes my dimples and hairy legs. But she says my constant optimism, sense of humor, and gentle spirit are what *really* turn her on. Giving themselves to their man is often a very personal thing for women.

Slow and Sensual

Women usually like to begin the dance slowly with lots of warm-up and connection time. The woman's brain often multitasks better than the man's—but can grow distracted more easily, too. She may take longer to fully enjoy the moment. Slow and more sensual characterizes the feminine approach. After this unhurried engagement occurs, the woman may then enjoy more direct and active involvement.

Remember Chantal's memory of the beach with its romantic sensuality? If they get married, Tyson's exciting memories of their honeymoon will probably be typical of most husbands: "We did it in ten different places." Chantal's memories, on the other hand, might be: "The cool satin sheets and anticipation of that first night, the feel of the bubble bath together, and going back to the room after looking into his eyes for two hours over a romantic, candle-lit dinner!"

Always Changing

The female sexual dance is to a variable beat. Men try to anticipate the woman's next move or the direction of the relationship, but this often doesn't fit with the complexity of female sexuality. Successful relating to a girlfriend or spouse cannot be determined by formula. Men might need plan A through E (or maybe Z!), gracefully shifting from plan to plan without getting defensive or pouting. Boyfriends can't look at this as "trying to get lucky" with some type of physical affection. Instead, they should simply enjoy the moment in the dance. Their women may need to provide some honest coaching on the nuances of feminine response. For example, Ty shouldn't expect that a box of chocolates will lead to a passionate kiss every time just because Chantal responded that way the first time he gave them to her.

Righteous Flirting: Enjoying the Dance

We define *righteous flirting* as men and woman affirming another's gender sexuality. When we bring up the concept of righteous flirting, people respond, "I thought flirting was manipulative teasing; how can it be righteous?" Worldly flirting involves giving someone attention *for your own selfish gain*. By contrast, righteous flirting gives attention *for the purpose of relating to and building up another*. This type of interaction has an important place in opposite-sex relating. Righteous flirting takes place in all three types of sexual relationships— Connecting, Coupling, and Covenanting—although the type of relationship will dictate how it's played out in each.

The Art of Righteous Flirting

Righteous flirting makes sexuality and the intimate dance of desire come alive. While many singles understand theoretically what we mean by righteous flirting, some express difficulty in actually feeling the freedom to truly enjoy the opposite sex. This may be especially true for those who (like both of us) grew up in more conservative faith traditions. For those who need more reassurance, here are a few of the essential elements of righteous flirting:

- a heightened sense of masculinity or femininity, becoming more aware of our gender sexuality and its power
- an awareness of God's image in men and women, enjoying the soul-sexiness of the other person
- lighthearted playfulness and uninhibited interactions, not taking oneself too seriously but instead enjoying the feelings of attraction
- conversational bantering with playful give-and-take
- nonverbal connecting such as eye contact, smiling, and appropriate, healthy touch

Styles of Righteous Flirting

Be careful that your flirting doesn't become harmful. Flirting to manipulate another sexually or merely to satisfy your own selfish erotic desire or ego needs distorts the dance of desire and leaves the other feeling used and abused. Setting wise boundaries in each of the following three types of relationships along the Relationship Continuum Bridge will ensure both individuals are affirmed and enjoy the benefits of righteous flirting.

Connecting: I have two women with whom I really enjoy righteous flirting: my five-year-old granddaughter and my eighty-five-year-old mother-in-law. My granddaughter, Caitlyn, knows how to tug at her papa's heartstrings with looks and feminine wiles, her laughter, her playfulness, and her obvious cuteness. She's still learning the difference between righteous and unrighteous flirting as she sometimes tries to manipulate her papa. My mother-in-law grew up in the Old South, an only daughter with four brothers. She enjoys men and makes me believe I can walk on water. Each of these females knows how to affirm my sense of masculinity.

Chantal and Tyson met through an activity at their church. Their eyes locked when Chantal walked in that first night. Righteous flirting began by enjoying each other's laughter and experiencing opposite-sex companionship with innocent erotic overtones. They resisted fanning the flames of eros each felt and avoided instant Coupling. This was particularly healing for Chantal, who was still raw from a prior broken relationship. Both sensed potential in the relationship but instead created appropriate intimacy in Connecting through playful flirting without any further expectation of the other.

Coupling: Righteous flirting takes on a richer tone when a couple's allure and romantic interests are engaged. Sexual surges add zest, with conversations and looks more lingering and erotic—yet still respectful. Righteous flirting in Coupling builds a foundation of self-confidence and vulnerability to become his woman or her man. The danger of using one's sexiness to manipulate is very real in Coupling. Chantal was used to men falling all over themselves, captivated by her cute figure and feminine manner. With Tyson, she determined to clean up her dance of desire and to *build him up* as a male friend rather than manipulating him into sex. She came to value healthy flirting as she focused instead on affirming him.

Covenanting: Have you ever seen the couple in their eighties at your church as he opens the door for her and gives her those gentle touches? Their flirtatious looks and tender love truly inspire. Adams and Eves at any age are fun to watch, but older couples bring a special meaning to righteous flirting. They know each other's bodies and spirits well, yet the dance of desire continues to create meaning. Probably the greatest danger to their relationship will be if they ever lose their ability to playfully flirt and forget to treat each other's gender differences with honor and lightheartedness.

Protecting the Dance of Desire

Protecting the dance of desire deserves our wisest and most loving efforts. Together, single adults can give new meaning to righteous flirting as they seek to protect one another. Keep in mind that *if you aren't presently Coupling or married, the Creator expects you to be focused on gender rather than erotic relating:* "Treat younger men as brothers, older women as mothers, and younger women as sisters, with absolute purity" (1 Timothy 5:1–2). God calls us to be our brother or sister's keeper sexually throughout our Connecting, Coupling, and Covenanting. The following sections are directed to each gender: first to women, then men.

Women Protecting Their Brothers

Know your own strength and his sexual turn-ons. In the dance of desire, men are quite visual as they tune in to bodies and run with sexual cues. They are more simple and direct than women.

Don't tease or manipulate. You can easily abuse your sexual power by offering more than should be delivered in Connecting or Coupling. Using your sexuality to get a man to do something he might not do otherwise is manipulative and selfish.

Dress and sit modestly. Sitting immodestly and leaning over so you are exposing underwear or skin are cues to your brothers more powerful than you can comprehend. Your female parts (navel, legs, breasts, waist, hips, genitals, undergarments) create mental images that excite men and require deliberate choices on his part to maintain sexual integrity.

Ask for honest feedback from close male friends about what items in your wardrobe may cause unnecessary struggle for men. If they're honest, they will tell you. But if they do, will you be brave enough to throw out a favorite blouse or skirt if it will help a Christian brother maintain sexual integrity? While men are always fully responsible for what they do with the thoughts in their head, women *must* take responsibility for the role they play in providing any unnecessary erotic stimuli by their inappropriate dress or behavior.

I remember a mom who brought her fourteen-year-old daughter into my office. "Can you help me teach Jessie the difference between being feminine and being seductive? She wants to wear micro-miniskirts and clothes I think are inappropriate in public." I started by comparing Jessie's outfit to her mom's: "Look at your mom's sweater. It shows she has a nice figure but doesn't make your eyes go directly to her breasts. Her skirt outlines her hips and legs. As a man, I can enjoy that without wondering what else is under the skirt. Jessie, your skirt is so short that unless you keep your legs crossed, your panties show. Your low-cut top draws my eyes directly to your breasts." From there we went on to discuss the intensified effect of such outfits on the hormonally driven boys in her school!

Monitor erotic touches. What may be a friendly touch to you might be a turn-on to a man. You may reply, "But I'm just naturally a touchy-feely person." We're not saying you should stop all touching. Everyone needs touch, especially single adults who are often touch-deprived. However, use wisdom and be aware of creating erotic arousal you don't intend.

Men Protecting Their Sisters

Know your own strength and her sexual turn-ons. Failure to do this can cause much hurt in your relationships. Men, women need you to operate with sexual integrity and love. Many times over the years, female clients have told me I was the first man with whom they'd ever felt safe. What a gift to keep sexual boundaries and communicate clearly with the women in your life.

Control your sexual desire and visual nature. Keep from constantly scoping out breasts and other female body parts. Honor women as people rather than treating them as sexual objects. Think with your head and not your hormones. The most seductive women are often the very ones who are really hurting with deep unmet soul needs. God needs you to help them heal and grow—not get sexually involved with them.

Don't manipulate or play on the heart. Understand the sometimes hidden messages of intimate behaviors, such as giving gifts and seeking someone out for special consideration. Every woman desires to feel special with emotional connection.

Keep clear communication about your intentions and the level of relationship you want.

Be cautious when paying focused attention to women. Such attention carries deep meaning and can unknowingly create erotic arousal and attraction in women. Two hours spent at Starbucks in deep conversation may give off mixed messages and stimulate romantic interest. Just as visual cues turn a man on, genuine empathy and being a strong male figure may cause your female friend to surge sexually. Don't shy away from such empathy; just be intentional about protecting her heart by maintaining clear boundaries as to the nature of your relationship so she won't misinterpret your actions.

Monitor caring touch and affection. A masculine hug or gentle touch is a wonderful thing to a woman. However, some may interpret more than you intend from such a hug. As with empathy and focused listening, women can be quite sensitive and cued in to touch. For non-coupling relationships, steer away from long hugs, caressing, cuddling, or touching near erogenous zones (genital areas, inner thighs, neck, waist area) to prevent your caring touch from being confused with something erotic or romantic. Don't be afraid to minister to a woman's touch needs, but always keep thoughtful boundaries in place.

Connecting through the Dance

And so the dance of desire goes on, with men and women protecting and inspiring one another through intimate relationships. Understanding that God created us with differences to reveal diverse aspects of his character gives us an appreciation for the fascinating (and at times even peculiar) interactions between the genders. For some, avoiding the opposite sex might seem the safest road for coping with the sexual ache. But, by God's design, quite the opposite is true. As you'll soon discover, connecting with the opposite sex is actually an effective way to scratch the loneliness itch.

Eleven

Guy-Girl Connecting

Scratching the Loneliness Itch
with *Vickie L. George*

Principle:
Express your sexuality through healthy connecting with both genders

Jodie came to counseling wondering if she could possibly create and maintain a good male friendship. Unless they saw potential for romance, guys didn't seem to want to connect with her. She longed for their compliments, listening ear, and masculine perspective. In Josh's last three relationships, the women quickly "fell in love" when he simply wanted to be friends—at least early on. He was also frustrated that others assumed that just because he and a girl were spending time together, they were an "item."

Now that you have a better appreciation for the masculine, the feminine, and "the dance," let's talk about the connecting friendships both Jodie and Josh so much desire. Without skills to intimately connect, you can't possibly develop a friendship into a healthy romantic relationship. *All* successful coupling relationships begin as connecting friendships—even blind dates and online matches. Making erotic romance the focal point of a new relationship without first establishing a genuine companionship all but guarantees you'll flame out when the intoxicating feelings fade, ultimately leaving your loneliness itch unscratched.

133

Distorted Connecting through the Years

Of the three types of relationships—Connecting, Coupling, and Covenanting—we spend most of our time in connecting friendships, whether we're single or married. From birth, many learn significant distortions in both same-sex and opposite-sex intimacy. All of us begin learning about connecting relationships early in life, most often from observing others. Parents, stepparents, and extended family play a large part in our early perceptions about same-sex and opposite-sex relationships—for good or for bad.

Some lessons were verbally spelled out; others were more "caught than taught." A young girl whose stepmom takes the time to watch her "dance recital" in her Cinderella dress quickly learns that what she has to offer the world is special and desirable. Yet a girl whose uncle molests her may learn the distortion that she must give of her erotic sexuality to please men and to become a person of worth. A young boy whose grandfather teaches him to fish or catch fireflies learns early how mutually enjoyed activities can be used to create enjoyable relationships. Yet he quickly learns to hide his feelings from others when, after he scrapes his knee, his mother sternly warns him, "Big boys don't cry."

The schoolyard is a notorious source for negative messages related to Connecting. Within peer groups, sharp words of non-acceptance from other children may cut deeply into a child's sense of self as he or she isn't invited to a party or is chosen last for a game of soccer. For many, fearfulness in same-sex Connecting has its roots in these formative years, laying the groundwork for a distorted sense of one's own gender that lies at the heart of many who struggle with gender distortion.

Children who've suffered relational wounding prior to puberty may be propelled toward a desperate pursuit of acceptance from their own gender group. Consequently, this may serve to begin (or cement) an erotic attraction toward same-sex peers at the onset of puberty. But for the majority of children, middle and high school will be a time for serious investigation into what the *opposite sex* is all about, often leading to greatly distorted intimacy skills.

Having never been taught to connect in healthy and respectful ways, many rely on trial and error as their primary learning tool. Through much relational drama, some will successfully learn to connect with the opposite sex. Others will be scarred by heartless rejection or manipulation. Distorted lessons of unhealthy sexual identity are often carried into adulthood and haunt many for life: fear of women, hatred of men, narcissistic male dominance, erotically manipulative femininity, and isolation from the opposite sex. Some will isolate themselves in Internet porn or romantically oriented chat rooms, favoring pseudo-relationships rather than risking the pain of complicated relationships in the real world.

Perhaps your past has left its marks on you. If you feel the weight of past baggage, you may need help in laying it down. Most people aren't objective enough to work through it on their own. Some who try turn current and future coupling partners into guinea pigs as they attempt to "work things out" in such relationships. A far better approach is to enlist a mentor, pastor, or Christian counselor to help you see more clearly how to grow and heal from your past into a healthier present and future, learning to develop healthy intimate friendships.

The Relationship Continuum Bridge

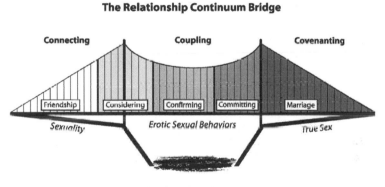

Beyond Distortions: Maximizing Friendships

From our Relationship Continuum Bridge, you can see the two types of interaction in connecting relationships: Connecting between friends (two people who aren't considering a romantic relationship) and Connecting between two people who are *considering* a romantic relationship but have yet to define an exclusive relationship as a couple (even though they may have "gone out" on any number of dates). Most friendships never become romantic. Both married and single adults need supportive male and female friends. Opposite-sex friendships will look different for marrieds than for singles, given the distinct roles and protective boundaries between spouses and friends. However, both are necessary to experience community as God intended. Single adults especially value their married friends who meet some of their needs for opposite-sex interaction and affirmation. My colleague Vickie and I (along with our spouses) have many single friends whom we nurture, yet always within appropriate limits. Wayne (Vickie's husband) and I open doors and extend small courtesies to our single female friends, while Vickie and Catherine (my wife) encourage and admire our single male friends.

Regardless of whether you remain single or someday marry, healthy Connecting with both genders is critical to creating community and scratching the loneliness itch. To isolate your relational experiences to only one gender (same or opposite) is to unknowingly isolate yourself from one of the two aspects of God as he makes himself known through the community of our Christian brothers and sisters. As counselors, we're often saddened the Church doesn't do a better job teaching men and women to create genuine friendships with each other and to enjoy "the dance" together. Unfortunately, our previous examples of Jodie and Josh remain more the rule than the exception.

Intentional Connecting becomes even more important if God has given you a desire to someday marry. Connecting relationships serve as the proving ground for opposite-sex relating. You weren't born knowing how to relate with the opposite sex—it's all learned. Unfortunately, many of us are still learning as adults to develop healthy opposite-sex friendships. Even if you had excellent role models growing up, creating your own opposite-sex peer relationships as an adult takes practice. Yet the effort is important because of our need for both same-sex and opposite-sex friendships as healthy single adults.

Women Inspiring Their Brothers to Connect

Ladies, intentionally doing the following for all the men in your life can make a real difference in their masculine sexuality. You can't comprehend your ability to bring out the best and the worst in a man, whether he's dealing with sexual surges, working through sexual attractions, or trying to find a friend or lifetime companion.

Give respect. Even more than women, men need to feel competent and be truly respected. Respect can be given in a variety of ways: praising his effort, being considerate, recognizing his strengths and accomplishments, asking him for help, and valuing his opinion. Tactful responses and loving coaching go a long way in building up his self-esteem so he continues initiating and protecting. Need more courtesy from him? Respectfully ask for it, giving examples if needed. Don't like his kissing? Gently coach him in what you *would* like. But beware: men won't stay in relationships with those who put them down or constantly nag.

Clearly communicate. Remember that men are simpler than women and more immediate in their interactions. They don't operate well with assumptions that they should "just know what is going on." They value clear communication, especially romantically. Jodie carefully stated her feelings and intentions to Ralph when he called wanting to turn their friendship romantic. She had to be respectful but clear to prevent hurting his feelings.

Receive and be responsive. Even though they want to initiate, men sometimes have difficulty risking rejection. Demonstrate appreciation for and encourage their initiative. I still remember how my wife enthusiastically accepted the opportunity to take a country dancing class with me in the early days of our relationship. I took more risks initiating after that.

Men Inspiring Their Sisters to Connect

Men, make a conscious decision to do the following for all the women in your life. You can make such a difference in the well-being and the quality of intimacy experienced by the women you know. They value and long for your healthy masculine attention.

Protect, defend, and honor. Women appreciate protection that gives them a sense of safety. Small courtesies such as walking on the street side of the sidewalk, opening doors, and offering to help with heavy objects can create feelings of security. Every woman welcomes someone standing up for her and defending her against attack—a knight in shining armor.

Honor her through small gestures that communicate your consideration of her.

Openly communicate. Women need to hear your masculine heart. Being open with your personal opinions and feelings can make such a difference in a woman's feeling safe and close to you. Risk self-disclosure, especially of your feelings. Not being your usual private self won't come easily, but it will help create genuine intimacy and build satisfying female friendships.

Make them feel special. Giving a woman your undivided attention makes her feel special. Try talking with her *without* doing something else at the same time (like watching TV or typing an email). Noticing and responding to her needs also go a long way; but it doesn't count for much if she has to ask or remind you. One of my single female friends was feeling especially down. A male friend noticed and told her, "You must have forgotten how beautiful you really are." This attention pulled her out of her mood. Listen attentively, give thoughtful gifts, and above all, take time.

Additional Tips for Connecting Friendships

Healthy, intimate Connecting lays the foundation for healthy, intimate Coupling. Here are a few more suggestions for making same-sex and opposite-sex friendships more rewarding:

- Develop your supportive community over time. Don't get too desperate. Great friends aren't forged overnight. Best friends grow from casual friendships that develop further when you make the time to share more intimately.
- Invite your friends to help you transform your isolation, insecurity, poor communication skills, depression, weight gain, or guilt.
- A key to great communication is empathy. Learn to step back from your own feelings and opinions and determine to walk in someone else's shoes.
- Don't focus on your considering relationship to the neglect of your other friends. After the breakup, do you really want to grovel back to your old friends because you completely neglected them during your "hot and heavy" dating relationship?

Expand Connecting Friendships

Single adults can utilize their connecting relationships to prepare for future Coupling and Covenanting. Here are some ideas many singles have found helpful over the years.

List-Making (Desirables and Non-Negotiables)

Each time you connect with someone of the opposite sex, you have the opportunity to explore the characteristics you're looking for in a future coupling partner. What's her denominational preference? Is he introverted or extroverted? Is she more active or sedentary? Is he organized and on time or more spontaneous and carefree? What are her personal strengths and weaknesses? Could you deal with his idiosyncrasies in a marital relationship if he *never* changed?

Qualities such as integrity, respectfulness, attractiveness, responsibility, and trustworthiness are characteristics we would all likely desire in a potential mate. Your unique personality may desire other qualities as well, such as someone who is funny, smart, outdoorsy, playful, steady, adventurous, artistic, outgoing, personally challenging, or has a love for sports or travel.

Observing these character traits up close before the interference of romantic involvement can be highly advantageous to your *learning about yourself* and the kind of person you're ultimately looking for. At the online relationship website eHarmony.com, Dr. Neil Clark Warren uses two categories: "Must Haves" and "Can't Stands." Similarly, we suggest you create your own list of ten to fifteen *non-negotiables* (things you either couldn't live with or couldn't live without in a covenanting partner) and another list of ten to fifteen *desirables* (things you would love to have but won't be deal-breakers if you don't find them). Whatever the method, it's important to clarify what you're looking for *before* getting into a serious romantic relationship. Once the flames of romance are ablaze, objectivity tends to go right out the window.

I (Vickie) made a list in my journal of things I was looking for spiritually, emotionally, mentally, physically, intellectually, and vocationally. I used this as my overall framework and filled in specifics as I learned more about myself and what I desired in a future mate. For instance, under "emotionally" I included

139

such characteristics as warm, good listener, sensitivity toward others, and a servant's heart. As a married woman looking back, I'm still amazed at how my husband fits the characteristics on my list. Of course, it took *twenty years* to find him, but he was worth the wait!

Letters to Your Future Mate

Here's an interesting exercise for maximizing connect-ing relationships (especially for more feelings-oriented folks): buy some stationery and write letters to your future mate. In them, talk to him or her about your dreams and struggles, your sexual ache and the anticipation of its fulfillment, and the many things you hope to someday share together. Write about the character traits you desire and admire most. Sort through how you desire to encourage them and to help them steward their true potential. Be open with your feelings and expectations. Keep your letters private from your coupling relationships until your covenanting partner finally arrives.

Tracey Casale, author of *Saved for My Beloved: Love Letters to My Future Spouse* (yet to be published), shared with us an excerpt from one of her own love letters from a few years back:

> You cross my mind frequently and often I pray for your beloved soul. I have been learning to love you faithfully, prior to even knowing you by name. I will do my best to love you fully and live in such a way that I have a full self to give to *you*. I am reminded as I write you under these stars tonight and as I hear the waves brushing gently against the shore side that *you* are the one I will make a full gift of myself to, only you. You will have my whole heart, mind, body, and soul. Please know that my writing you now is the only way I know to love you, to give *you* my love now. Love, T.[1]

Letters such as Tracey's can bring many benefits to your connecting friendships. They may:

- assist you in evolving a model for what you desire in a future mate
- help you maintain your perspective in connecting relationships and to not rush into Coupling as you wait

for that right person, choosing to meet your emotional needs in healthy ways rather than "using" another person

- give you resolve for protecting your soul virginity during Coupling as you set appropriate boundaries and wait for your Adam or Eve
- help you practice a transparent and open style of communication that will serve you well in a future lifetime covenanting relationship
- potentially be presented as a one-of-a-kind gift to be read by your future spouse—when the time is right

Searching for Mr. or Mrs. Right

What we've mentioned thus far illustrates the importance of same-sex and opposite-sex friendships. Through them, you will lay the groundwork for a significant secondary benefit for Connecting: finding those of the opposite sex you would *consider* marrying. Of course, finding that person of your dreams can be downright exasperating. With so many unhealthy and immature men and women to sift through, where will you look to find the godly mate of your dreams? The local bar isn't likely to have what you're looking for as a Christian single. However, there *are* good alternatives to consider.

For example, I (Vickie) met my husband, Wayne, at a gym that was part of a church program. We knew each other as friends for four years before our first date. Seeking non-romantic friendships *before* pursuing romance is a good idea. Even if at first sight you find someone sexually attractive, *pursuing a friendship first will allow each of you to know the other as a person before exploring them as a lover.*

Singles' Group at a Local Church

Many Christian single adults enjoy participating in the singles' group of a medium- or large-sized church. While this is certainly a valid place for finding a quality mate, make sure to carefully evaluate your motives when considering this option. Too many singles attend a church with an active singles' group *for the sole purpose of finding a mate.*

The purpose for a local church community is to provide a spiritual family for each believer, where you can mutually serve one another based upon your unique spiritual giftedness (see 1 Corinthians 12:18). If you immaturely select a church based mostly on its potential for finding a spouse, you'll likely bounce from church to church and miss the greater benefits of a stable, supportive church family. Yet if you have the proper motives, a church singles' group can be a great place to meet *people*— including a potential mate.

Online Romance

Online matching services have become increasingly popular among Christian singles. The success of such websites comes from their ability to remove some of the guesswork out of finding a potential mate by screening out candidates who don't "match" your personality or stated values. They allow single adults to meet people (either locally or literally across the world) who never would have met otherwise. I (Michael Todd) have personally found eHarmony.com a great resource not only for meeting potential coupling partners but also for learning more about myself through the unique process of communicating with good matches.

But a word to the wise: don't always believe everything you read in someone's online profile. Too many Christian singles have "fallen in love" with an online persona only to feel differently when interacting with them in person. If your heart gets involved before you know them for who they really are, your brain will fill in the gaps with the way you *want them to be* rather than the way they really *are*.

Face-to-face time is critical for building intimate relationships. Statistics reveal that only 7 percent of human communication is the *actual words* we say (or type); 38 percent is the *way* we say them (voice inflection, pitch, volume—things you can only interpret by hearing their words); and 55 percent is *nonverbals* (hand gestures, "looks," facial expressions—things you can only interpret in person). *Therefore, the Internet alone only communicates 7 percent of the whole story.*

Even taking an online relationship to the telephone only bumps the communication experienced to 45 percent. This level of experience still misses over half of the critical information you need to accurately assess a potential partner. If you're pursuing an online relationship, do yourself a favor: get to know the other 93 percent of the person as quickly as possible *before* you decide he or she is the partner of your dreams. If you prefer moving more slowly, then by all means do whatever is necessary to protect your heart from becoming involved too quickly in the meantime.

Be aware of one more pitfall to dating services. Their stated goal is to create coupling relationships. However, it's our belief such relationships can only work if you put this goal on hold temporarily and allow each relationship to begin as a connecting friendship. The crucial connecting process is too often bypassed, with needed information gathering and skill building short-circuited. When you match with someone of interest, resist Coupling too soon. Purposefully linger on the "Connecting side" of the considering stage as you focus on building non-romantic companionship.

The "Friends and Family" Plan

Think of the people who know you best. They have a network of people they know, too. Could they possibly help you take some of the guesswork out of finding a suitable soul mate? Many single adults neglect developing this potential networking gold mine. One group of female friends started having "share the wealth" parties and inviting all their male buddies. The only downside to this method is that the feelings of the "matchmaker" may be hurt if things don't go as they'd hoped. However, thanking them for the introduction and telling them you will "take it from there" can help. Of course, purposing to become friends with a potential partner before becoming romantically involved will also help.

Volunteerism and Similar Passions

A trait many single adults look for in a potential mate is common interests, such as interest in similar charitable work. Becoming involved in something you care passionately about (overseas missions, singing in the choir, mentoring children, working a political campaign, etc.) will allow you to rub shoulders with others who have similar interests.

These are but a few ideas for ways quality Christian singles may be found. If you desire marriage someday, actively (not desperately) seek a quality partner and allow God to help you mature into your attractive best. "He who finds a wife finds a good thing" (Proverbs 18:22 NKJV). Of course, the same holds true for finding a husband. The question then becomes: as a Christian single adult, how should I pursue a potential soul mate?

More than Just Friends: "Considering" as Preparation for Coupling

Throughout life, you will develop many connecting friendships with the opposite sex. However, some of these connections will spark chemistry that's undeniable. Your heart may skip a beat with romantic attraction when you're around a certain person. At some point, you make the deliberate transition to begin "considering" something more than a friendship. This typically begins when you go out on a first date, which we define as two people who get together for the purpose of getting to know one another better—*with the knowledge that some level of chemistry exists between them.*

As you remember from our Relationship Continuum Bridge, we've put "considering" under both Connecting *and* Coupling. What distinguishes a Connecting type of considering from a Coupling type of considering is an *intentional definition* to the relationship. In Connecting, no defined relationship exists other than friendship, and there is no commitment to romantic exclusivity. You might go on double dates or dates by yourselves, but "going on a date" doesn't define a coupling relationship.

You will notice that we use the term "dating" more literally than most. Dating is merely a word describing what you are doing (going on dates), *not* who you are as a couple. Understood this way, dating means you are "considering" the other person as potentially more than a friend. However, unless there is serious consideration of marriage and an exclusive dating arrangement has been agreed upon, it's still Connecting —you are not yet a "couple."

What about hugging, kissing, or hand-holding while considering in a connecting relationship? Rather than legislating specific behaviors, we offer two stewardship questions for you to consider: (1) What is the *purpose* or *meaning* behind such behaviors? (2) Are these behaviors about being *compassionate* or *passionate* toward one other?

John feels kissing Suzanne good night after their dates is merely his way of compassionately saying, "Thanks for a wonderful evening." However, Suzanne views this as too passionate for her. But to her, a good-night hug feels compassionate and like an expression of thanks. This once again illustrates the importance of dialogue about expectations and perceptions in Connecting.

Remember too that erotic sexual behaviors should begin *only* in Coupling. This protects budding relationships from cementing too quickly, with little or no commitment between two people. We believe that only when a couple is committed enough to define an exclusive relationship—willing to consider the *possibility of future marriage*—can such erotic behaviors appropriately be expressed and enjoyed.

So here are some tips on remaining a connecting relationship while considering, allowing more time for growth before deliberately moving into Coupling:

- no physically erotic activity, allowing touch to remain more appreciative than affectionate
- less time alone as a couple, with more time in public places and in group activities with friends
- less face time, as you limit daily contact and extensive phone time
- allow intimate data-collecting and self-disclosure to occur naturally as the relationship develops over time

God's Culturally Radical Approach to Finding a Soul Mate

The steps for finding the man or woman of your dreams begin with a godly worldview. A *worldview* is simply the lens, filter, or beliefs through which you see the world around you. Scripture shows us God's viewpoint and has much to say about how to pursue your soul mate: "It is God's will that you should be sanctified: that you should avoid sexual immorality; that each of you should *learn to acquire a wife* in a way that is holy and honorable, not in passionate lust like the heathen, who do not know God; and that in this matter no one should wrong his brother or take advantage of him" (1 Thessalonians 4:3–6, italics represent NIV alternate translation).

The word *sanctified* means "holy" (literally, "set apart") and carries a similar idea as the Hebrew word for "virgin" in the Old Testament. God's purpose and desire for you is a holy or "set apart" soul virginity. This means avoiding "sexual immorality"—avoiding behaving sexually in ways that cause destruction to God's design for both premarital and marital relationships.

Acquiring a wife (husband) in a holy and honorable way (or, if you were already married, the way you should continue "acquiring" your spouse) becomes a radically different process as a Christian. How does the world go about this? By grabbing selfishly in "passionate lust"—raw erotic pleasure—with little consideration for the other person and without an understanding of the unconditional love distinctive of God's own character.

A Christian's pursuit of a spouse should be distinctly different from this. We are called to avoid wronging our brother (or sister) or taking advantage of him. What does this mean for the present and the future? *As a believer involved in any premarital relationship, you must assume the other person does not belong to you—that he or she may ultimately belong to another.* Until marriage vows are exchanged, there are *no* guarantees. You should operate as if you are getting to know another man's future wife or another woman's future husband. Treat them with the respect you hope someone is showing *your* future spouse, and avoid inappropriate erotic behavior—sexual immorality—that selfishly "takes advantage" of what rightly belongs only to their future Adam or Eve (v. 6).

Acquiring a spouse God's way requires a different worldview than that of our culture. In addition to this passage, Scripture encourages among other things that we marry only Christians (2 Corinthians 6:14) and pursue relationships with honesty in communication (1 Peter 2:1), encouragement (Ephesians 4:29), forgiveness (Ephesians 4:32), and a servant's heart (Matthew 23:11). Finally, it teaches us to pursue unconditional love, which expresses itself in patience, kindness, protection, trust, hope, and perseverance, while doing what's necessary to avoid envy, boastfulness, rudeness, selfishness, and anger (1 Corinthians 13:4–7).

146

At the point when two people know each other well, experience chemistry, and sense the possibility of spending a lifetime together, they will engage in a discussion about the relationship (some people call this "defining the relationship," or DTR). Ideally, the man would sense a need to initiate the discussion. But most important is the need for *every couple to engage in a DTR discussion and make a deliberate decision to dedicate themselves to an exclusive relationship.* They prayerfully pledge to seek God's will in exploring a possible lifetime commitment. In short, they choose to define themselves as a *couple.* An exciting and passionate new pursuit begins.

Part 3:

Intimacy with God's Possible Soul Mate

Twelve

Coupling

Chemistry or Purposeful Choices?
with Vickie L. George

Principle.
Evaluate your potential soul mate while learning about yourself, disciplining erotic behaviors, and making deliberate decisions

"We've been a couple for a long time, but I'm still not sure what he really wants." We hear so many stories of extended dating and lack of commitment that it's almost amusing. Of course, it's not amusing to the partner involved. How much more data can you collect after seven years of Coupling? We're not encouraging impulsivity, just stressing the importance of deliberate decisions.

"Suppose one of you wants to build a tower. Will he not first sit down and estimate the cost to see if he has enough money to complete it?" (Luke 14:28). The process of constructing a great marriage parallels the planning and construction of a beautiful building. The different stages within Coupling reflect the critical importance of following a plan. Our goal isn't necessarily to get you to "buy into" every aspect of *our* model for building a godly coupling relationship; rather, it's to *challenge you to become more thoughtful, prayerful, and intentional along the journey.*

When One and One Make Two

In the previous chapter, we described the basic difference between Connecting and Coupling. Coupling is an exclusive relationship between a man and a woman who have made an intentional decision to evaluate each other as potential lifelong partners. Priority is placed on knowing each other more genuinely over time. It's about being up front and honest about feelings and your interest in a future relationship. In this manner, Coupling becomes "basic training" for Covenanting, or marriage. Only those who are truly pondering this ultimate destination are ready for Coupling. This fact significantly limits the number of relationships we would label as "couples."

Here's another observation. Adolescents are generally *not* prepared for the responsibility of caring for a family and children, as they are more concentrated on schooling, friends, and establishing psychological independence. They're also still tethered to their family financially and, therefore, unable to provide for the needs of themselves or another. Only *adults* are ready for Coupling or Covenanting. And note this too: under our model, erotic sexual behaviors are only considered appropriate in Coupling. Though not likely popular with many teens and even some single adults, such a model frees connecting relationships from experimenting with a "force" they are not yet fully ready to handle with maturity and purpose in the early stages of relationship discovery.

Erotic sexual behaviors are intended by God to move a relationship over time toward marriage and true sex, revealing a more complete reflection of intimacy. Logically, then, these behaviors were *not* intended to be a part of Connecting. This explains our rationale for placing erotic behaviors within Coupling only (more about godly decision-making and "where to draw the line" for Coupling in chapter 14). As you might expect, a great deal of difference exists between a couple in their early stage of exploration and a couple preparing to walk down the aisle. The three stages of Coupling help us explain this.

The Three Stages of Coupling

To better grasp a typical progression along the Relationship Continuum Bridge, consider Bill and Tina. They initially met when Bill first visited Tina's church last year. At that time, they began Connecting as friends with no real consideration of anything else. They talked almost every Sunday, got together with other church members for activities, and even served alongside each other on a mission trip to Mexico.

The Relationship Continuum Bridge

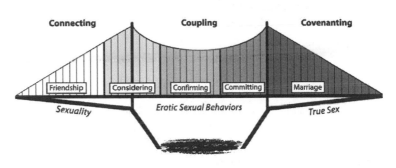

However, a few months ago, Bill began to think about Tina a bit differently. He's always felt she was attractive. But as they've come to know each other better, Bill has been impressed with her spirit, love for life, and desire for godliness. They also have many interests in common, including reading, attending concerts, and a love for the outdoors. So Bill asked Tina for a date to attend a local Christian concert, an invitation Tina eagerly accepted.

Considering

With this step, Bill and Tina have transitioned from merely connecting as friends to considering—*but still as a connecting relationship.* Bill won't pursue her physically other than a good-bye hug, and Tina won't feel any internal pressure to figure out what she'll do if he does. The reason is simple: they're both aware of the Relationship Continuum Bridge, having discussed it on their first date. Each is clear on the "rules of engagement" in Connecting, and each has agreed to respect the other. They simply desire to know each other in a deeper way by spending more focused individual time together.

Considering isn't just about hanging out or doing activities together. Getting to know another person more intimately takes a bit of planning and forethought. If you always see movies together, you'll only get to know the other person's preference in film. If you're trying to know someone better, consider "the Five Fs":

Food: One way to create opportunity for meaningful conversation is sharing a meal, especially when a restaurant has nice ambiance and isn't too noisy. Ask relevant questions of each other, from surface questions such as, "What's your favorite restaurant?" or "Tell me about your family" to more personal and emotionally connecting questions such as, "If you could do anything in life over again, what would it be and why?" Such curiosity not only reveals helpful information about their personality but also gives you a glimpse into their ability to carry on "below the surface" conversation.

If you're not the world's greatest conversationalist, take heart. The Appendix has an assortment of questions you might consider for starters. They will encourage getting to know someone in a more well-rounded sense. You might consider taking the list with you on one of your dates to stimulate conversation.

Fun: Invite the other person to do things you enjoy. Find out what sports, hobbies, and interests he or she enjoys and share them together. Not only will you learn about the other person, you'll also have fun—and maybe even find a new hobby.

Friends: Invite him or her to join a small group of your friends to do something together and vice versa. Observing how another behaves when they're with their circle of friends can yield great insight about their "true colors." You might also try doing a work project together, such as yard work, grocery shopping, or a community cleanup effort.

Future: What does he or she want to accomplish in the next year? Five years? Twenty years? How would he or she answer the question with regard to career, family, friends, where to live, how to play, and ways to volunteer? This can reveal much about the relationship's long-term potential. Different visions for the future will eventually yield divergent paths.

Faith: Does he or she profess Christian faith? Does his lifestyle evidence or betray this profession? What does she believe about church, Scripture, and a daily walk with God? If one of you holds faith as central to daily life and the other merely gives it lip service, the relationship can only go so far. Some value differences are indeed "deal breakers" in Coupling—this is one of them. Don't fool yourself into believing you can "change" them. People *choose* to change. They aren't manipulated into it, no matter how lovingly it's done.

Such spiritual differences are okay as a connecting friendship. Perhaps your godly influence will encourage them to seek after God. However, allowing your emotions to lead you into Coupling will only spell disaster. This truth forms the backdrop for Scripture's warning not to "team up with those who are unbelievers" (2 Corinthians 6:14 NLT).

After two months of delightful dates to a concert, a movie, the zoo, and a few dinners, Bill is more impressed with Tina than ever. Bill suggests their next date be at a quiet restaurant where they can talk, followed by a walk around the nearby park. His intention is to have a discussion about the future of their relationship and whether she is as interested as he in an exclusive coupling relationship—*built upon the intentional exploration of moving their budding relationship in the direction of marriage.* At dinner, he tells Tina his desire to become a couple—choosing to date no one else—and that a desire to go on a date with another from this point forward would be acceptable only after a joint decision to return their "considering" from Coupling back to Connecting.

With a grin, Tina agrees. As they further define their relationship while walking around the lake, their considering moves from Connecting to Coupling. Bill and Tina openly discuss what their newly agreed-upon relationship will look like as they have their "defining the relationship" (DTR) conversation.

We believe couples should be intentional about not only the direction of their relationship but also its boundaries. In a manner of speaking, "good fences make good couples." With expectations discussed up front, each can relax and enjoy the relationship, knowing what to expect from the other.

In fact, if you're presently Coupling, we encourage you to share this book with your coupling partner. Reading it together can create an opportunity for dialogue about becoming more intentional in these areas. Perhaps you need your own DTR discussion.

What areas should couples define? In addition to defining the relationship as "exclusive" and intentional toward consideration for marriage, couples need to place clearly understood limits on specific erotic behaviors, recognizing the godly need for avoiding all forms of intercourse, mutual orgasms, and lust (Hebrews 13:4; Matthew 5:28). No other issue has the power to ruin a good couple as having poorly defined sexual boundaries (for more on this, see chapter 14).

For the guys, let me (Michael Todd) simply spell it out for you: you're in sort of a "lose-lose" situation. Either you'll have a conversation with her ahead of time about physical boundaries and run the risk of "killing romance," or you'll fly by the seat of your pants trying to figure out whether she'll accept or reject your "move" on her. Depending on her emotional state that day, this second scenario will earn you the label of either "not interested" (if you don't move fast enough) or "pushy" (if you move too fast). Trust us: it's healthier and godlier to run the risk of "killing romance" by bringing it out in the open. At least she'll respect you for it—and respect goes a long way in Coupling between two healthy people.

And a note to the women (from Vickie): Speak up! Be responsive to a guy who's trying to (1) define the relationship, (2) move the relationship forward, or (3) exit the relationship. He needs your input. Don't be afraid to tell him what you like and don't like. But don't expect him to "just know," "figure it out," or "read your mind." This can lead to very mixed messages. He will likely assume you're on the same page if you remain silent. Learning this communication skill now will help you greatly in a future marriage, too.

How will you know when you're ready to take a relationship from Connecting to Coupling? Here are a few questions to consider:

- Are you sure you *really* want to be married to anybody in the first place?
- Are you ready to commit to an *exclusive* dating arrangement?
- Have you already established a successful *friendship* with this person?
- Are you willing to proactively define the relationship (DTR) *prior* to entering into Coupling?

- If this person turns out to be all you'd hoped, are you prepared to marry them *in the near future*?
- Does this person pass the test of your *"non-negotiables" list* for a life partner?

Only if you can answer yes to *each* of these questions are you truly ready for Coupling.

Confirming

Bill and Tina have now been Coupling for over six months, and it's getting serious. Each has talked openly about a possible future together. They pray for God's discernment, together and individually. Now each must risk full disclosure with the other—a time for honest sharing of their private hopes and dreams as well as their secrets and closely held fears. This is the often-neglected (but crucial) stage of Coupling known as *confirming*.

At this point, an official announcement of engagement *does not* occur. Some have called this stage of Coupling "engaged to be engaged"—*a time each partner willingly places all their cards on the table and risks abandonment for the chance at a relationship in which they are fully known.* The couple wades into the deeper emotional *reality* of becoming "naked and unashamed"—genuine intimacy—of which the act of true sex is but a *picture.* Any secrets thus far held from the other need to be shared during this stage. To the degree secrets are held back, to that same degree fear will exist on the part of the secret-holder and (if it's ever found out) mistrust on the part of the secret-discoverer. Keeping secrets is a lousy way to start a lifelong commitment.

The couple may need to plan a day trip (or several such trips) somewhere quiet to create a safe place for discussion. Of course, this depends on how much of their true selves has already been disclosed over the natural course of the relationship. No question should be off limits: prior sexual relationships; STDs; homosexual attractions; past abortions; debt; financial instability; expectations about children, child-rearing, in-laws, and frequency of sex; denominational preference; gender roles in marriage. If it's important to one partner, it's important for the couple's future survival to bring it into the open for honest discussion. This is also a great time to read and discuss together a book about sex in marriage, such as my *Celebration of Sex for Newlyweds.*

Movement from the confirming stage to the committing—or engagement—stage should not take place until each partner has fully disclosed everything and is satisfied the other has done likewise. The confirming stage is also the best time for premarital counseling from a pastor or Christian counselor. Confirming couples allow the idea of being married to settle on them as they actively sort through the joining of two lives. Premarital counseling presents a great opportunity for the counselor to teach skills, affirm strengths, and expose weaknesses in the relationship. When premarital counseling is prioritized at this stage of the relationship, the couple has time to either work through the issues or call off the relationship without undue burden of social or family pressure on either partner.

For example, discovering through counseling a partner's past substance abuse or struggle with same-sex attraction allows for more energy toward resolution than waiting for such counseling until the committing stage—*after* the invitations have been mailed and everyone has high expectations for the couple. Delaying such intimate discovery not only will place undue pressure on the couple ("Do we postpone the wedding? What will we tell our guests when they ask?") but also may cause irreparable damage to the relationship itself.

While working on this chapter, we (Michael Todd and Vickie) saw an incident in our local news that eventually became a national obsession, further illustrating this need for full disclosure in the confirming stage. Everyone has heard stories about "cold feet," but this bride-to-be literally disappeared days before the wedding, causing heartache to family, friends, and an entire community—not to mention national embarrassment. We wonder if such an incident would have occurred had the couple sought complete honesty through disclosure and premarital counseling while confirming their relationship.

The confirming stage should purposely involve the couple's family and support network. One premarital counseling model involves parents/stepparents with the couple in a session, formally asking them to bless their child and to help launch the couple into their new commitment. My (Doug's) twenty-year marriage to Catherine came after my first marriage ended in a painful divorce. This time around, I got *everybody's* opinion— including my parents' formal blessing.

One final thought about the confirming stage: just because a couple takes steps toward potential marriage doesn't mean they should feel *obligated* to become more physically intimate. On the other hand, some couples may have legitimate reasons for making a "calculated movement" toward greater physical intimacy while posting new, clearly marked "stop signs" for the more intimate erotic behaviors (see chapters 14 and 15). We sometimes worry if couples *aren't* having trouble keeping their hands off each other, requiring them to discipline their sexual surges. But lustfully indulging an erotic buzz differs significantly from having an unselfish desire to create true intimacy—while still struggling.

If you're a couple struggling in this area, you might consider the discipline of *erotic fasting*. I (Michael Todd) think you'll agree that in immature Coupling, increased physical intimacy sometimes leads to *decreased* verbal intimacy through communication. Too much emphasis on the physical can also lead to the neglect of other important dimensions of the relationship, including mental, social, emotional, and spiritual intimacy. Couples miss out on getting to know each other and enjoying social interaction in a more well-rounded sense. Too much emphasis on the physical may also lead to decreased objectivity about the relationship's potential, as the physical dimension consumes a more significant part of the time invested in the relationship.

Fasting from specific or all aspects of physical intimacy for an agreed-upon period of time can be a valuable tool in Coupling when used for the purpose of maturing a relationship. Respecting a more conservative limitation on physical intimacy for a time may benefit your coupling relationship in a number of ways:

- You could discover a new depth of love for each other (that is, you might find reasons you love your partner *besides* the erotic behaviors shared).
- You might discover your relationship becomes so empty without the erotic behaviors that you're forced to work on improving other areas of the relationship (mental, social, emotional, and spiritual intimacy), making it healthier and stronger.
- You might decide to reconsider how healthy the relationship is or isn't. The erotic intimacy might have been the only glue holding it together. In this case, the

relationship should prayerfully be discarded either temporarily or permanently.

Erotic fasting in a romantic relationship also reminds you to depend upon God to meet your deeper intimacy needs. This is a good thing, especially since he is the only true source for getting your deepest intimacy needs met, anyway. Real intimacy is more than erotic physical expression. Remember, *Coupling is basic training for marriage*. Deliberate and unintended erotic fasting also occur at times even in marriage (sickness, post-childbirth, physical separation, periods of not getting along). Voluntary periods of premarital erotic fasting can prepare for such occasions in marriage. Fasting from erotic behaviors will not only teach you delayed gratification but will also reveal if the person you're considering marrying can delay gratification. What a great character quality to know about your partner *before* getting married!

Committing

Having become familiar with each other's strengths, faults, failures, goals, and dreams, Bill and Tina realized each held assumptions about their future marriage they were previously unaware of. Thankfully, they'd pursued full disclosure prior to formal engagement, allowing them the extra time necessary to work through their issues toward greater understanding, acceptance, and resolution. Though it wasn't easy, they are convinced taking the road less traveled gave them not only a deeper appreciation for each other but also a head start on success in their first years of marriage. With more resolve than ever, Bill and Tina moved into the *committing* stage of Coupling.

Because much of the difficult relational work has already been done, their engagement will be merely as long as practically needed to coordinate actual wedding plans—sending invitations, selecting dresses and caterers, planning their honeymoon, and so on. This shortened engagement can be a significant benefit for couples who've already chosen to do the hard work in the confirming stage. Having discussed what their joint lives will look like, the committing stage can be all about the *practical* steps of joining two lives together: opening a joint checking account, initiating steps toward merging two households, and the like.

The committing stage is also a time when priority should be placed upon "grieving and cleaving." No, this is not a typo. Men especially have a genuine need for *grieving* the loss of singleness. Reduced independence and potentially reduced financial freedom are real losses that must be grieved to successfully "leave" the benefits of singleness and "cleave" to the good (but different) benefits of marriage.

For women, this grieving is typically a bit different and less pronounced. Women may grieve felt differences in their female friendships. Their single friends may view them differently, back away, or even become jealous. Couples will benefit from talking together with seasoned marrieds who can give advice from their own experiences, allowing the soon-to-be-marrieds to learn from their own successes and mistakes

I Didn't Promise You a Rose Garden (or at Least Not One without Thorns)

Please be aware that the references to time spent in each of the three Coupling stages by Bill and Tina are simply one couple's experience and are in no way shared to set any sort of precedent for other couples. Each relationship will be unique in its own progression through the stages of Coupling. However, following our model for Coupling should at least reduce the time required for the committing stage. It also should significantly reduce your risk of a broken engagement and greatly reduce the likelihood of an unhealthy marriage by heading off problematic romance before the "point of no return." In addition, such intentional progression in Coupling encourages the biblical view of stewardship of your partner, leading to a greater sense of respect for him or her.

While following our model should help circumvent some of the common problems couples face along the road toward marriage, it's by no means foolproof. You will still need to watch for potential trouble at every turn. Christians have a common spiritual enemy who seeks to infect even the healthiest of relationships (1 Peter 5:8), using our own sinful desires as a means of creating opportunities for sin and heartache (James 1:14–15). Knowing some of the common viruses ahead of time will help inoculate your relationship against being destroyed from within.

Thirteen

Viruses That Infect Healthy Sexual Relationships

Principle:
Guard yourself against common destroyers of healthy intimacy

The scary uncertainty of a virus certainly gets one's attention —stirring up fears of something incurable. After personally suffering through several nasty computer viruses, we decided this might be a better metaphor for those common distortions of healthy sexual relationships. Relational viruses aren't so much like incurable STDs as they are computer viruses— disruptive and destructive, demanding immediate attention.

We hope you will learn about each virus and set up good "antivirus protection." Avoiding a nasty virus is always wiser than having to decontaminate your heart and relationships from a particular infection.

Disrespecting Your Own Sexuality

The Virus

The slang word *dis* (meaning to disrespect) strongly emphasizes a person's intrinsic need for justice and self-worth. Single adults fall into many traps of sexually dissing themselves and their relationships, such as sexual bartering, poor body image, and the seemingly endless number of sexual games and myths. In an earlier chapter we discussed the importance of accepting and disciplining your sexual desires rather than ignoring or repressing them.

I once asked a single female friend about her first date with a gorgeous hunk: "Did you kiss him?" I knew about her conviction to refrain from erotic behaviors in Connecting, and I wondered how she'd handled someone very attractive to her. She admitted she had kissed him, then defensively stated that he'd given her a great evening and had dropped over a hundred dollars on dinner. I sarcastically threw up my hands and declared, "So now we're into bartering for your sexual favors?" We both laughed, but I knew she'd gotten my point.

Winston Churchill once told a story of a young lady at a dinner party. Sitting across from her was an older gentleman whom she'd never met. Over the course of the meal, the gentleman quietly slipped her a note asking if she would go to bed with him for ten thousand pounds. She blushed and nodded in agreement. When they had gone off to a bedroom, the gentleman asked, "Say, would you go to bed with me for *ten* pounds?" In disgust the young lady said, "What kind of girl do you think I am?" The older man responded, "We have already established what kind of girl you are; now we are just negotiating over price."

What kind of games do you unknowingly play that cheapen your sexuality? In the above story, the older man was just as guilty of disrespecting God's intent for sexuality as the young lady. What myths and distortions have you bought into as a single adult: You *have* to have sex? Sex is simply *recreation*? You use erotic sexuality as *relational currency*?

Guys, do you enjoy and find strength in your masculinity? A man can disrespect his masculinity by lusting over pornography, which degrades both genders as sexual objects. Ladies, are you satisfied with your body image? A woman can easily disrespect herself by comparing her body to the Madison Avenue standard. As a female colleague once stated, "Why do women's breasts seem to come in only two sizes—too big and too small?"

God's Antivirus

Maintaining soul virginity and deeply honoring God's gift of sexuality are the ultimate antidotes for disrespect. Accept God's declaration that you are "fearfully and wonderfully made" (Psalm 139:14). Your body and sexuality are beautiful to him, and you can take great pleasure in that truth. Single adults can practice affirming each other's soul-sexiness in ways that don't require bartering of sexual favors, big or small. Singles can also create honesty in relationships and prioritize open communication. Pledge to be held accountable by close friends when you're in a coupling relationship. Encourage them to give you honest feedback about areas where you may be operating under common myths that might destroy your relationship.

Indulging the Sexual Rush

The Virus

Although sexuality is similar to other body functions (such as eating), God placed it in a category all its own. Something is terribly wrong when sexual interactions are reduced to simple recreation and physical titillation. God's great plan is about deep intimacy, not creating erotic buzzes and rushes. Remember, the sexual verbs are not "score" and "get some" but "relate" and "connect."

Burt hired a life coach, trying to make sense of his sexuality. He wondered why he was "doing it more and enjoying it less." His coach asked him a profound question: "What does your sexuality mean to you?" He quickly replied, "Fun." This response evolved into dialogue about God's purpose for creating erotic sexual activity to be experienced only in the context of committed relationships. Lovemaking can remain sensual and satisfying in the covenant of marriage in part because two lovers grow increasingly intimate over a lifetime. But pursuing lovemaking only for the sexual rush always demands bigger and stronger buzzes to maintain the high. This type of erotic pursuit is the stuff sexual addictions are made of —an addiction with very similar characteristics to that of crack cocaine.

God's Antivirus

Sexual surges are more than hormones; they reflect an intrinsic desire to be intimately connected with another being. Creating a three-dimensional intimacy of body, soul, and spirit takes sexual interactions beyond the buzz. The "crack" of sexual addiction comes in many forms. It may develop from compulsive use of online chat rooms, pornography, trashy romance novels, one-night stands, serial relationships, or even a codependent style in relationships. If you're concerned about such patterns in your own life, consider reading *Healing the Wounds of Sexual Addiction* by Mark Laaser (for men) or *No Stones: Women Redeemed from Sexual Shame* by Marnie Ferree (for women).

Meeting Non-Erotic Needs Erotically

The Virus

Every person has a legitimate need to be hugged, held, comforted, affirmed as sexy and special, and deeply valued. These are *not* erotic needs. Healthy single adults must find godly ways to meet these needs through appropriate non-erotic means.

After John's mother died, John simply wanted a woman to hold and comfort him. Not having close female friends, he decided the only way to accomplish this was to find a girl and become sexually involved. Megan felt unattractive and unappreciated. Sex with guys was her way to feel lovely. Both John and Megan are eroticizing non-erotic needs.

God's Antivirus

Learn healthy ways of giving and receiving non-erotic physical affection within single friendships. In singles' workshops, I often teach single adults to enjoy healthy touch through the use of conga lines and shoulder rubs. We practice hugging in ways that feel safe and comfortable for both genders. Christian brothers and sisters can give verbal compliments and help each other feel special and sexy. *Most of our sexual needs can be met in non-erotic ways*, but it takes creativity, skill building, and encouragement. In God's sexual economy, erotic sexual behaviors and true sex are much smaller boxes within the much larger box of sexuality. Using erotic behaviors to meet non-erotic needs is like putting out your birthday candles with a fire hose. Not only is it overkill, it will do significant damage to the cake in the process.

166

Hoping Instant Erotic Connecting Creates Instant Intimacy

The Virus

Our society values the quick, easy shortcut. Contrary to Hollywood's portrayal, instant chemistry and erotic behaviors *neither cement commitment nor ensure long-term romance.* So many single adults ache for intimate closeness and hope erotic behaviors will provide the answer. April enjoyed feeling "in love." She also feared that if she wasn't sexual with her boyfriends, they would leave her. Yet because they were enjoying true sex outside of the long-term protection and commitment of marriage, it was only a matter of time before her boyfriends could want more and leave for another relationship.

God's Antivirus

True sex doesn't create intimacy. It only enhances intimacy that's already present when enjoyed within its proper context, the commitment of a covenant marriage. In the naturally tentative place of a premarital relationship, true sex may provide erotic energy but will never create commitment, safety, or healthy intimacy. If you're genuinely interested in fostering greater intimacy in your premarital relationships, read carefully chapter 15—devoted entirely to the need for creating greater intimacy that's healthy and balanced. Physical (erotic) intimacy is only one of the five spokes of the Wheel of Sexual Intimacy. Focusing on this spoke alone will all but guarantee relational imbalance and sabotage.

Turning Intimate Friendships Romantic

The Virus

Asking the question "Why can't we be lovers since we're already friends?" is potentially a great way to kill a solid friendship. Romance and erotic involvement dramatically alter a relationship. In his singles' Bible study, Dave was the only guy among fourteen women. He was attractive and funny, but he was already in a coupling relationship. He developed some significant friendships there and grew close to several in the group. He thought of these girls as great friends and nothing more—until his girlfriend broke off their coupling relationship.

Dave didn't handle it well. Suddenly his Bible study friends became "dating material." He'd never really wanted to date any of his friends, but many were attractive and he enjoyed them. Why not? After only a few months, however, he was on speaking terms with so few in the class that he no longer felt comfortable attending. He hadn't done harm on purpose, but he found out the hard way that it's tough to date the entire Bible study group and remain comfortable in that setting when things don't pan out. This is especially true when your only rationale for dating someone is believing a great friendship must be a predictor of great romance.

God's Antivirus

Instead of being desperate on the rebound, Dave could have used a buddy to talk some sense into his head. Great friends won't make healthy marriage material *just because* they are desperate or "surging." If you decide to pursue Coupling with a close friend, *go slow* and talk it through early in the process. Many friendships are not destined for romance and marriage. Be intentional in your actions, making your erotic desires subordinate to wisdom and concern for the interests of the other person.

Spitting into the Wind: Ignoring and Distorting Boundaries

The Virus

How fascinating that some people think, *If I spit into the wind, I'll avoid the natural consequences.* Do they really believe it won't fly back and hit them? They think they can go too fast sexually, spend the night at his apartment, drink too much, and indulge in erotic sexual behaviors "just for fun" without any negative consequences.

Sexually whole single adults enjoy the freedom of making wise choices rather than ignoring or testing God's law of

168

sowing and reaping. This requires setting up healthy boundaries in a relationship. To say you will never engage in deeper erotic expression unless you're "in love" with someone (whatever that means!) is *not* setting a real limit. Erotic sexual feelings and genuine love for another are easy to confuse when you're in a long-term relationship, alone in his apartment at 2:00 a.m., or just plain lonely.

Be honest with yourself about this virus. What creates chemistry and makes you feel "in love"—the desire to find someone similar to or different from your parents? A certain body type? Four margaritas? Sheer loneliness? When the fickle winds of emotional change come blowing, you're potentially setting yourself up for a world of hurt.

God's Antivirus

A sign of true maturity is *the ability to postpone immediate gratification for long-term gain.* Every connecting and coupling relationship needs healthy stop signs for certain erotic behaviors. The concept of stop signs will be further developed in the next two chapters, but a healthy stop sign can be an identifiable behavior (such as touching beneath clothing) that you *deliberately* choose not to engage in. Put real stop signs in your relationships and not just the vague "in love" rule. Being "in love" is a great feeling we hope you experience in Coupling. But this feeling comes and goes for most couples, even those with successful long-standing marriages. The feelings are nice to have, like icing on a cake. The cake mix, however, is made from ingredients like commitment and deliberate choices based on common values and direction in life. The consequences of premarital true sex (pregnancy, broken hearts, STDs) go far beyond the feelings of love. Shouldn't the decision to engage (or not engage) in erotic sexual behaviors be made intentionally and rationally based on our real values and long-term aspirations rather than merely upon the "heat" of the moment?

Repressing Your Sexuality

The Virus

Although most viruses tend to err more on the side of Christian hedonism, repression is just as dangerous to healthy relationships. We could relate countless stories of couples that go something like this: A couple tries to control their sexual surging by complete repression. They never kiss, hold hands, or even allow their knees to touch while watching a movie. Even the thought of such things is met with internal messages of being "wrong" or "dirty." The couple eventually gets married, and on their wedding night find themselves alone for the first time with the expectation they will undress in each other's presence, touch intimately while naked, sleep in the same bed, and experience blissful intercourse. To their surprise, they can't because the script in their minds is still saying "wrong" and "dirty."

We aren't suggesting you need to "practice" certain erotic behaviors for your honeymoon. What we *are* saying is that it's extremely important to recognize and honor your erotic desires in Coupling and not just suppress them. Yes, these desires do need to be monitored, disciplined, and possibly managed outside the relationship (such as with an accountability group). But to simply ignore or rebuke these desires altogether can reap an unwanted harvest.

God's Antivirus

David (one of our single adult contributors) has always enjoyed having his ears rubbed. Though he wouldn't be comfortable with this in a connecting relationship, he enjoys it in coupling relationships. For him, it's an erotic behavior that doesn't fall on the wrong side of his own personal boundaries.

Some books on dating suggest that relationships should effectively go from Connecting straight to Covenanting—that no one should kiss or express any other erotic behaviors before you say "I do." We're not suggesting everyone *should* kiss before they marry—refraining from doing so could be a wise plan for some couples to discipline their sexual desires. But when a particular couple sets boundaries around more conservative erotic behaviors (such as kissing), they should make certain

170

they are *motivated by godly, heartfelt values rather than religious traditions, something they've read, or repression.*

Honestly recognize that erotic sexual *feelings* exist in both Connecting and Coupling. Treat them as components that need to be enjoyed and disciplined in your relationship, much like money and time. Eros (or romantic love) is part of the coupling process. Invite it to your coupling party. Instead of ignoring it, think through how to enjoy it within limits that are consistent with your values.

To avoid these common sexual viruses successfully, you will need to prioritize honest dialogue with your coupling partner on how to set limits within your unique relationship. This will require a balance of law and grace. Stop signs will need to be thoughtfully placed throughout your coupling journey. Such practical boundaries will serve as a strong antivirus to help protect your budding relationship from harm, promoting loving intimacy.

Fourteen
Law, Lovetouching, and the Bikini Line

The Proverbial "How Far Can I Go?" Chapter

Principle:
Discipline erotic behaviors using heart-directed boundaries motivated by law *and* grace

Some of you probably bought this book just for this chapter and even started reading it first! All of us would love an easy-to-apply Christian formula to guide our erotic sexual behaviors. This chapter may leave you frustrated because it won't give you a legalistic, cookie-cutter approach to sexual purity. It's got to be a soul thing. We hope you've heard enough of our heart to understand that "how far can I go?" isn't sufficient. That common question shows our humanity and by itself is rather selfish and immature. Instead, we should dig deep into our souls and ask, "How do I grow, stay pure, and help my partner become more sexually whole—building a solid foundation for great lovemaking in future marriage?"

However, the "How far can I go?" question is still an important one to consider. In fact, it brings us to a very practical concept. While it's true that Christians do live under grace (from a heart motivated by godliness), we still need a measure of law (i.e., "How far can I go?") to keep our sinful, selfish hearts on track.

The Tension between Law and Grace

Join us on an imaginary trip. It's November, and you're on your way from the East Coast to a reunion with a friend in Colorado. Bone-deep with fatigue, you've seen enough of Kansas and Interstate 70 to last two lifetimes—when suddenly you realize you're significantly exceeding the speed limit. What should you do?

Your body is crying out for rest and to be done with this tedious journey. You know you're on a deserted stretch of highway with no speed traps. As a mature Christian, though, you immediately slow down because you know laws are there for your own good. You don't want to run the risk of hurting yourself or another motorist regardless of whether the cops are out. Right?

Wrong! The pedal's to the metal. On this lonely night, the spirit of the speed limit law evades all conscious consideration. This story humorously illustrates a common dilemma. We need rules and guidelines. Unfortunately, we often also need others to help us keep them. Otherwise, our human hearts have a tendency to behave both immaturely and irresponsibly, even when our deepest values are consistent with such laws.

But here's the catch: when it comes to our erotic sexual behaviors in adult relationships, the "sex police" aren't out. Laws (God's regulating principles) related to sexuality can't really govern your behaviors unless they are self-imposed and *internally* motivated by your mind, will, and heart. They become guides you can choose to follow—or not.

The Rules without the Heart

Mark and Tiffany fell in love their sophomore year of college. They grew up in very conservative homes where sex was not discussed. The intensity of their erotic surges somehow seemed wrong. So they constructed rigid boundaries around their erotic behaviors. They thought they were doing well as they followed the strict guidelines set up in their former youth group—light kissing and hand-holding only.

Everything was great until Christmas vacation, when Mark went over to Tiffany's before heading back to school. The physical part of their relationship was fun and bonding. They spent lots of time together that night. To their dismay, their erotic behaviors went much further than either anticipated.

After that night, the couple resolved to shift back into the safe and rigid rules of the past. But when they were together, these rules seemed to fly right out the window. The cycle repeated itself again and again—breaking rules, redoubling their resolve, only to break the rules again. By the following spring, disillusionment with their lack of discipline brought them in for counseling.

After listening to their story, I made several observations about various topics we've addressed in previous chapters. Their relationship clearly had the virus of disrespecting their normal sexual desires. In their upbringing, rules had been set *without any explanation of their deeper purpose in protecting God's gift of intimacy*. Mark and Tiffany repressed their erotic sexuality rather than practicing healthy self-discipline of their sexual surging.

The Heart behind the Rules

The fact that Mark and Tiffany repressed their erotic sexuality didn't make their rules wrong. Scripture encourages us to set godly rules for inappropriate behavior. Laws are designed to pinpoint counterproductive behaviors and encourage us to see the heart of God and his plan for us: "Through the law we become conscious of sin. . . . I would not have known what sin was except through the law" (Romans 3:20; 7:7). Being wise stewards requires a couple to understand the *spirit* behind God's sexual guidelines that can help motivate the discipline of godly sexual behaviors.

Building mature attitudes based on the spirit of the law is quite different from simply outlawing behaviors and legalistically following the rules just because the sex police might be out. A key sign of adult maturity is the ability to keep rules and postpone immediate pleasure for long-term gain. Teens often think having sex will make them adults, when the opposite is actually a truer test of mature adult character.

Mark was surprised at how quickly sexual immaturity took over when they didn't relate deeper heart principles with their sexual rules. Scripture is quite relevant here: "Such regulations indeed have an appearance of wisdom . . . but they lack any value in restraining sensual indulgence" (Colossians 2:23).

Simply outlawing certain behaviors won't stop your sexual thoughts and behaviors from going outside the lines.

Pursuing the spirit of the law, I told Mark and Tiffany that I preferred the term *lovetouching* for sexual caressing. Romantic affection involves more than recreation or indulging sexual surging. *Lovetouching is a soul thing that implies the need for both the commitment of Coupling and a genuine concern for your partner.* Lovetouching guides behavior out of an attitude of respect for the other person and the relationship— incorporating tenderness, patience, consideration, self-discipline, and a desire to be connected and intimate. Such a viewpoint holds us accountable to a different ideal than petting, fingering, groping, and other demeaning terms our culture uses for sexual behaviors.

Mark and Tiffany appreciated the idea of lovetouching but were still discouraged they could violate their desired boundaries so easily. I reinforced the difficulty most singles have in being governed by the spirit of the law instead of merely the letter of the law. Sex police wouldn't miraculously appear, order them to stop, give them a ticket, or revoke their license—although that certainly might seem warranted at times. *A sexually mature courtship needs to combine law with the deeper reasons for that law.* That kind of motivation only comes from the heart and a deeper understanding of God's desires for genuine intimacy.

The Heart without Rules

Then there's the opposite problem. Keith and Traci's voices resonated with shame as they shared their pain. They'd been together at her apartment until 2:30 a.m. the night before and had once again been sexual in ways both knew were wrong. They asked for each other's forgiveness and had already sought forgiveness from their loving heavenly Father.

After listening to their story, I directly challenged them: "You've done some good work in setting godly boundaries. You also understand and believe in the reasons behind them. *You're simply choosing to disobey them.* You aren't allowing your boundaries to do their job because you deliberately ignore them."

Keith quickly replied, "But we're keeping better boundaries than we used to." Traci followed with, "We struggle with wanting to make better choices. We're just so in love."

"Nice try, guys," I responded, "but you are in my office because you're fearful of harming your relationship. You must *choose* to make some bold changes. Maturity isn't kissing passionately at 2:30 in the morning in her apartment. You aren't consistently observing your stop signs."

Posting Stop Signs

A *stop sign* is any behavior you choose, by the deliberate act of your will, not to engage in until you've reached a certain level of commitment in your relationship. These "symbolic behaviors" will help you discipline your erotic desires. Examples of stop signs might be no erotic sexual behaviors until Coupling (which we feel applies to everyone), no kissing after midnight, no hands under clothing, or no making out after a romantic movie.

The journey into mature sexuality is interestingly complex. Couples must firmly post *and* respect stop signs. Understand that stop signs alone are ultimately powerless without your mutually heart-driven choices—that's the respecting part. You'll need to develop character and a loving three-dimensional intimacy (body, soul, *and* spirit) while still respecting the need for law to serve as guideposts.

The Song of Songs beautifully tells the story of maturing Coupling and Covenanting. It also illustrates the wise use of an erotic stop sign. Three times in this story Scripture emphasizes the importance of not "awakening" or "stirring up" erotic passion before its time (Song of Songs 2:7; 3:5; 8:4). Single adults need to discipline their erotic surges by setting limits throughout the different stages of Coupling. Bottom line: you must serve as your own mature sex police.

Guard against being too simplistic in thinking through your stop signs. For example, you might be one of those single adults who chooses to wait until your wedding day to kiss, believing that kissing symbolizes a behavior that creates too much sexual intimacy in Coupling. But if you're cuddling on the couch watching a romantic movie and wondering how to ignore his erection, your choice not to kiss isn't helping you discipline your other erotic feelings and behaviors very well. Sexual maturity recognizes the complexity of sexual response in Coupling and the need for a variety of behavioral boundaries. The stop signs you post should reflect your deeper heart attitudes and must be chosen wisely for them to be effective in disciplining your sexual surges.

The Biblical Stop Sign of True Sex

Part of the reason you're reading this chapter comes from your desire to see what God says about erotic sexual activity, especially sex outside of marriage. Many of you are already having sexual intercourse or mutual orgasms with your partner. Because of the great confusion among Christian single adults on this subject, we want to take time to walk you through a simple (okay, so it's a bit complex) journey through Scripture to help you see why true sex belongs only within the covenanting relationship of marriage.

To help you understand why we're so firm on this particular stop sign, let's go back to the three-step inside-out model we developed in chapter 3. The steps we presented for understanding God's will about any specific life issue begins first with applying biblical passages that *directly* address the issue (step one). If none exist, then apply biblical passages that *indirectly* address the issue (step two). In some cases, you may need to seek out godly mentors or ministers to help you rightly interpret some of the biblical passages you find—or even to help you find them in the first place. If, after all this, the issue still remains *unclear*, then allow each believer to prayerfully settle the issue for themselves, consistent with their hearts and internal values and shaped by God's heart as seen in Scripture (step three). However, unlike the Bible's silence on masturbation, Scripture has *much* to say about what are inappropriate erotic behaviors for premarital relationships.

A Biblical Understanding of Sexual Immorality (Step One)

Hebrews 13:4 says the marriage bed is to be kept pure. It specifically mentions two groups of people who violate the purity of marital sexual intimacy: adulterers and the sexually immoral. When God's design for sexuality is distorted, strong words like *adultery* and *sexual immorality* emphasize how deeply the Father's heart is grieved. *Adulterers* refers to those who break their wedding vows by engaging in sexual intercourse with anyone outside their own marital relationship. Our English phrase "to adulterate" means to corrupt something pure by adding a contaminating element. Remember, God created human sexuality to help us understand genuine intimacy and to demonstrate his covenant relationship with his people.

Jesus would later apply the matter of adultery to the heart by including even *mentally lusting and objectifying another person* as a component of adultery (Matthew 5:28). God looks at the heart of your erotic desire to understand how you are using your sexuality. When you mentally lust after someone with whom God wants to give you a pure connecting or coupling relationship, you contaminate and adulterate something potentially beautiful in your life.

As for sexual immorality, the original Greek root word used in Scripture is porne, from which we derive our English word pornography. The New Testament interprets this Greek word by any of the following English words: sexual immorality, prostitution, fornication. Unlike adultery, sexual immorality is a broader term that can be used for any inappropriate sexual behaviors outside the commitment of marriage. It is also used regardless of an individual's marital status.

Therefore, Scripture is clear that we shouldn't commit adultery or engage in sexually wrong behaviors (*porne*, or sexual immorality). This clearly includes sexual intercourse but may include a variety of other erotic activities as well. Therefore, Hebrews 13:4 and Matthew 5:28 are direct passages we must live by. This is step one of the inside-out model. However, since Scripture doesn't give us specific examples of just what other kinds of behaviors "sexual immorality" might include, we're left to do some interpretation based upon the rest of Scripture.

Sexual Immorality through the Eyes of Scripture (Step Two)

We now seek to apply step two from our model, examining passages that indirectly address the issue. So how else *does* Scripture speak of sexual immorality and true sex outside of marriage?

Isaiah 1:18-23; Ezekiel 16:1-63—These passages refer to Israel's abandoning their worship of Jehovah God (whom they'd made a covenant to serve) to become a spiritual "prostitute" by serving other gods. The ideas of being unfaithful and breaking a vow are encompassed in the idea of sexual immorality. In sexual terms, this would amount to *sharing with someone else those sexual things that are intended only to be shared within the context of a covenanting relationship.*

Genesis 34:1-31 (especially v. 31)—This is a heart-wrenching story about a woman's rape. Her family became so angry at the perpetrator (and rightly so!) that her brothers referred to the incident as his treating their sister "as a prostitute" (v. 31), using the same root word used for "sexually immoral." In their view, Shechem (the offender) took something that didn't belong to him. Their sister's physical virginity was being intentionally set apart for her future husband. It didn't matter that Shechem was attracted to her (v. 3), even attracted enough to request his father to "get me this girl as my wife" (v. 4). *His future desire, intention, and even possible future marriage to her didn't matter. At the time of the incident, neither she nor her sexuality belonged to him.*

1 Corinthians 6:12-20—The apostle Paul warned the Corinthians that when they engaged in erotic sexual interaction with a prostitute, they weren't simply getting an erotic fix. Sexual intercourse united them with that person on a deeper level spiritually—as if they were married, or "one flesh" (v. 16). On the surface, Paul is talking about sex with a prostitute. Yet a deeper admonition is clear: *Don't engage in any inappropriate erotic sexual activity—especially the intimate becoming "one flesh" of sexual intercourse—with someone outside of a committed marital relationship.*

Ephesians 5:25-33—Becoming sexually one in marriage mirrors the covenant relationship Christ has with his bride, the Church. Sexual intercourse is both a metaphor for this spiritual reality and a physical sign that seals the earthly covenant of marriage. A person becomes part of Christ's bride with a deliberate decision to pledge his or her life to Christ. In the same way, the covenant of marriage pledges two people to one another, making them "one flesh" and sexually uniting them in true sex.

To summarize the above Scripture references, sexual immorality has *at least* the following characteristics: (1) erotic sexual behavior (2) between two people who aren't married to each other (3) that at least includes the lovemaking behavior of sexual intercourse (true sex). Also, (4) neither being "in love" nor having a future intention or pledge to marry seems to affect Scripture's perspective on the issue.

This understanding of sexual immorality should significantly impact your behaviors if you claim to be a follower of Christ. Many single adults in the confirming and committing stages of Coupling feel it's okay to enjoy all the benefits of married life (including sexual intercourse) since they are "going to get married anyway." This thinking contains serious flaws, since nothing can guarantee their marriage will actually take place. Thousands of engagements are broken each year by couples who at some point believed "without a doubt" they were getting married. *For premarital couples, the bottom line biblically is this: at least at this moment, you are not married —period.*

Here's another comment we frequently hear from singles: because of their love and commitment for one another, they believe they are already "married in the eyes of God"—even if they aren't yet married by public ceremony. This is terrible logic designed either to quiet guilty consciences or perhaps to ease their fear of commitment. If you're a couple *serious* about lifelong commitment, take our advice: exchange your vows publicly in marriage and allow your family and friends to hold you accountable for your promise to one other.

Allowing God's Heart to Guide (Step Three)

Now, you're probably still wondering, "What behaviors *besides* sexual intercourse are considered 'sexual immorality'?" Even after all of these Scriptures, we still haven't defined other specific behaviors (besides sexual intercourse) that can be destructive to your coupling relationship. Maybe you're saying to yourself, "So, we'll do our best to make good decisions. Right?"

181

Well, not exactly. We still must live in a way that's consistent with God's heart as expressed in Scriptures such as "Serve one another in love" (Galatians 5:13) and "'Everything is permissible for me'—but not everything is beneficial" (1 Corinthians 6:12). *Just because the Bible has no direct or indirect teaching against something doesn't necessarily mean doing it is healthy, godly, or even wise.* As we said earlier, "How far can I go?" isn't a mature and loving question. When asked by itself, it's usually based on selfish motivations. When singles are honest, this is the real question often lurking beneath the surface: "How much of what I'm supposed to reserve for the marital relationship can I selfishly experience now and still not cross the legalistic line where either God won't bless or we will suffer serious harm?"

This lack of clear direction doesn't necessarily mean God's heart bans *all* erotic sexual behaviors before marriage. A variety of sexual behaviors could be appropriate and healthy (kissing, deep kissing, lying together while watching a movie, lovetouching, etc.). For behaviors neither directly nor indirectly addressed in Scripture, you'll need to prayerfully search your God-directed heart attitudes and your unique coupling relationship. This is what applying step three of the inside-out model means. But remember: your body (and your erotic sexuality) isn't your own. It belongs to God and your future spouse (1 Corinthians 6:19–20; 7:4).

The Bikini Line

In God's sexual economy, all erotic behaviors are modeled after and build toward marital lovemaking. As Christians, we don't want to mirror a society that places such emphasis on genitality and orgasms even in premarital relationships. Instead, our values and behaviors need to reflect God's truth that true genital sex can only be fulfilling and complete with our Adam or Eve in marriage.

As you further sort through stop signs that will enhance and protect your coupling relationship, let us suggest the *bikini line*. We believe this valuable physical stop sign applies throughout *all* stages of Coupling and helps preserve soul virginity. The bikini line rule says that the parts of the body covered by a bikini (genitals and breasts) should be reserved for

182

Covenanting. Yes, this eliminates any type of mutual orgasms, whether manual or oral, under clothing or on top of clothing (sometimes known as "dry humping"). Another way of saying it might be, "If you don't have one, don't play with someone else's!" (In case you're wondering, this in no way gives permission for same-sex erotic behaviors). Other sensual body areas—such as neck, tummy, and mouth—will have to be enjoyed within the context of a growing coupling relationship and according to other heart-driven stop signs posted by each couple.

Remember, the bikini line isn't important simply as another legalistic rule to follow. It's important because it helps single adults protect one another's true sex from being misused outside of a covenanting relationship.

So what does the bikini line do for Mark and Tiffany and Keith and Traci in our earlier illustrations? It hopefully gives them freedom and safety, serving as a guidepost in their Coupling. That's what a healthy stop sign is all about. The sex police aren't going to arrest you for running a relational stop sign. Instead, you will need to choose wisely to refrain from counterproductive behaviors according to the spirit of the law. *You need to maturely recognize that if your hands or mouth stray over the bikini line (or some other stop sign you've posted), a type of erotic arousal is stirred up that frequently results in moving to mutual orgasm and intercourse—a place you don't belong in Coupling.* You also don't want to offend your partner's future spouse by taking something that doesn't belong to you—even if you "know" you're the future spouse.

Here's another viewpoint on the bikini line: imagine that having true sex as a single person can be equated with falling off a cliff into the Grand Canyon. The "How far can I go" question then becomes, "How close can I get to the edge of the Grand Canyon and still not plunge to my death?" Immature, worldly values are all about getting as close to the edge as possible without falling over. *Wisdom* calls you back from the edge to maintain a reasonable margin of safety—while still being able to enjoy the view.

Connecting and Coupling are invaluable preparation for marriage. Posting stop signs (and keeping them) will help you build the necessary skills of patience and self-discipline. Intercourse won't always be available in marriage, and God is teaching you now how to love erotically without true sex. An alarming number of couples have extramarital affairs their first few years of marriage because they've never learned covenant faithfulness.

Think back on Keith and Traci, who regularly violated their stop signs. What if God knew Keith was going to work closely with a very seductive colleague during his second year of marriage. The disciplines learned and practiced in Coupling would help him through such a tempting situation. Don't blow off these necessary lessons of courtship! Soul virginity applies even after you say "I do." You are learning to make the many difficult choices to preserve marital soul virginity now in singleness.

The Importance of Personal Responsibility

Suppose we told you the two of us (Doug and Michael Todd) left our Atlanta residences one morning and met at Stone Mountain, near our Georgia homes. We then climbed to the top of the mountain, where God gave us an official decree, written on non-rewritable CDs, about the bikini line. Further suppose that he not only gave this edict but also charted out *all* erotic behaviors with "age" and "stage of relationship" guidelines: at age twenty you could deep kiss with a romantic coupling partner, but hickies would be reserved for age twenty-one. Yeah, right! God does care about behaviors. But as we said before, he cares even more about your heart.

As you've probably figured out by now, we're not going to draw a line for you about whether each specific erotic behavior is appropriate or inappropriate within your own coupling relationship. We don't want to play judge and jury where Scripture isn't clear. True sex—which at least includes intercourse (oral, anal, vaginal) and mutual orgasms—we believe is scripturally out of bounds before marriage. We also highly commend to you the bikini line as a mature premarital stop sign that can protect both you and your future covenant partner (whomever he or she may be). For everything else, the line you need to draw depends on your heart and what the behavior means to you and/or your partner as you intentionally respect future marital lovemaking.

We believe all other erotic behaviors are left to the category of "disputable" (or personally applied) matters as described in

Romans 14:1–23. We ask you, dear Christian, to sincerely pray for the Lord's guidance regarding the variety of other erotic behaviors—then to rest securely in your decision. Ask yourself, "How does this behavior affect me and my relationship both with my coupling partner and with God?"

Once you've prayed it through, sought godly counsel (if necessary), and discussed it thoroughly with your coupling partner, confidently and playfully engage in the behaviors you've agreed upon without guilt or doubt: "Blessed are those who do not condemn themselves by doing something they know is all right. . . . If you do anything you believe is not right, you are sinning" (Romans 14:22–23 NLT).

You must take personal responsibility for whatever decisions you and your coupling partner ultimately make. Also, beware of needless comparisons with others. What may be counterproductive behaviors for you as a couple may be appropriate behaviors for your friends who come from a different background, or vice versa. Even depending on your heart attitude, the same behavior may be a sin on Monday because of your desire for a buzz but on Wednesday may be godly lovetouching because of your desire to communicate intimately with your partner.

Practicing Godly Stewardship

In an effort to be as practical as possible, here are a few final questions to ask yourself in the spirit of inside-out theology. If you're honest, these questions will likely encourage you to draw "the line" more conservatively than you might otherwise want:

1. Because you aren't yet married, assume your future spouse (whomever he or she may be) is going out on a date with someone else tonight. Where would you want that man or woman to set the erotic behavior limits with your future spouse tonight? Many single adults have never thought of such a question. Yet it only makes sense that *wherever you want the line drawn for that person in terms of erotic behaviors, you must be willing to accept this same limit for yourself presently in your own coupling relationships.*

For the remaining questions, think of a *specific erotic behavior* you're concerned about and ask yourself the following:

2. Would you regret having done this behavior if your current coupling relationship didn't ultimately end in marriage? Could you remain friends with this person without feeling guilty? How about with his or her future spouse?

3. Does this sexual behavior change the focus of your relationship from encouraging godliness to merely gratifying your own selfish lust? Is intimacy the focus, or are you merely indulging sexual buzzes and hormonal surges?

4. At the moment you engage in this behavior, does it stimulate you to want to carry your erotic expression to its ultimate conclusion—sexual intercourse? If so, it may be too arousing for you in Coupling and, therefore, too risky.

5. Are you "falling into" physical expressions of intimacy because the relationship is lacking in the area of sharing spiritual, emotional, social, and mental intimacy?

As steward of the sexuality God has entrusted to you, we challenge you to honestly before God ask yourself these questions when pondering which erotic behaviors are appropriate and inappropriate in your coupling relationship. Each of these questions may yield red flags you will want to give attention, as your own soul virginity may be at serious risk.

Bless you, friend. Erotic sexual intimacy brings many dilemmas and tough choices for couples who truly desire to walk before God in righteousness. We know this won't be an easy journey for you. However, your loving heavenly Father cheers you on. His desire is for you to create a fun, safe, and soul-satisfying intimacy that may one day lead to beautiful covenant lovemaking for a lifetime. But getting there requires *many deliberate choices* to keep your intimacy in balance and your relationship moving in a healthy direction.

Fifteen

Well-Rounded Intimacy

Maintaining Balance

Principle:

Develop balanced intimacy and sexual wholeness by slowly growing the five spokes of sexuality

We've been saddened over the years to hear various inadequate definitions for intimacy, such as "being in love," "hanging out," or simply "hooking up." For this chapter, we considered conducting a poll to define the word *intimacy*. We concluded this wasn't a very rich source of information; we would probably just get the same answers over and over again.

When asked to describe intimacy, people often assume they're being asked about either erotic sexual behaviors or true sex. As you now know, this is far too simplistic. This chapter will help you develop and understand the five most important facets of mature and loving relationships. Our sexuality involves all five of these "spokes": spiritual, emotional, mental, social, and physical. True intimacy cannot thrive over time without a balanced development of all five areas.

The Wheel of Sexual Intimacy

The movie *The Fast and the Furious* appealed to an entire generation of guys who live for fast cars. There's something about taking an ordinary, street-legal car and turning it into a muscle car that draws out the Vin Diesel in all us guys. You can outfit a car with a huge 400-plus horsepower engine, quad exhaust, racing stripes, and a spoiler, but no such car would be complete without a set of mag wheels. Such racing tires are a great illustration for the process of developing a well-disciplined sexuality into a well-balanced intimacy in relationships.

The Hub: Sexuality

Throughout this book, we've developed the understanding that *sexuality* and sexual surging propel us into relationship with others and with God himself. When a single adult pursues relationship with someone of the opposite sex, the wheel of sexual intimacy begins to rotate around its sexuality center, causing the relational vehicle to move forward. The Wheel of Sexual Intimacy applies to all three types of relationships along the Relationship Continuum Bridge: Connecting, Coupling, and Covenanting. *We create connecting relationships through gender (non-erotic) sexual expression and create coupling and covenanting relationships through both gender and erotic expressions of sexuality. But regardless of the type of relationship, sexuality is the common hub.*

The Five Spokes: Expressions of Sexuality

Reaching outward from the hub of sexuality are five different types of sexual expression: spiritual, emotional, mental, social, and physical. These five "spokes" make up intimate wholeness, containing both erotic and non-erotic expressions. Each spoke helps to develop healthy connecting, coupling, and covenanting relationships. The spokes aren't completely independent from one another but complement and interact, creating a balanced wheel.

Balance is crucial in developing well-rounded intimacy in relationships. When one spoke is larger (or smaller) than the rest, the wheel becomes out of round and will eventually cause extensive damage—not only to the wheel (sexual wholeness) but potentially to the vehicle itself (the relationship). Couples must grow *slowly* in each area, especially since the excitement of new romance has the tendency to grow certain spokes too quickly. Our fast-paced society serves only to make matters worse. This process will require couples to patiently and gently grow each of the spokes into a complete wheel supportive of balanced intimacy and sexual wholeness.

The Tire: Balanced Intimacy and Sexual Wholeness

All five spokes are needed to sustain the tire's overall integrity. This is a wonderful description of intimacy involving spiritual nurture, emotional warmth, mental stimulation, social playfulness, and physical touch. This five-spoked intimacy produces a mature *sexual wholeness*, reflecting God's intimate best. When properly maintained, balanced intimacy gives the relationship a tread to potentially last a lifetime.

The Five Spokes of Intimacy

In chapter 12 we discussed how Bill and Tina wisely evolved their coupling relationship by avoiding their past mistakes—though they still hit a few bumps along the road from time to time. "Strongly connected but not always smooth" might describe their journey through the three Coupling stages. Like most couples, they struggled with certain spokes more than others. They quickly realized their journey required growing together in each of their problem areas.

Spoke #1: Spiritual

Spiritual intimacy ultimately refers to building a personal love relationship with God. This process includes many of the suggestions we made in chapter 6. Neither Bill nor Tina came from a religious background. Both enjoyed their spiritual growth after initially coming to faith as young adults. Yet they were a bit startled to find themselves sexually surging after intimately praying together one night. A wise friend helped them see their spiritual intimacy had created a special closeness they would have to guard maturely. Sharing hearts and enjoying God's presence together can be tremendously bonding.

Spoke #2: Emotional

Though women often tune in to their emotions more closely than men, neither gender finds it easy to be consistently emotionally expressive. Real *emotional intimacy* lets the walls down to become "naked and unashamed" emotionally. Building trust and safety become important factors. Strong feelings (anger, fear, jealousy) need to come out at times to work through conflict as a couple. Most adults have a skill deficit in the area of expressing feelings in healthy and God-honoring ways. Jesus encouraged us to become like children (Matthew 18:3–4). While he was referring more to recognizing our utter dependence upon God, becoming like children also involves freedom from inhibition to express our hearts, whether in pain, joy, excitement, or curiosity. *Depth of intimacy grows in proportion to your ability to express your feelings.* This requires practice and taking risks to be vulnerable with one another.

Spoke #3: Mental

Mental intimacy is often overlooked. However, neglect this spoke and your intimacy wheel will certainly be out of round. Sometimes the word *mind* is used as a synonym for the soul. Examples of mental intimacy include dreaming about and planning for the future, use of humor, making deliberate choices as a couple, and engaging in stimulating discussions on topics of mutual interest. Playful banter, though also including the emotional and social aspects of intimacy, stems from our minds and imaginations.

Renewing your mind (Romans 12:2) and changing unhealthy thought patterns can also help ensure growth in this area. Tina came out of unhealthy sexual attitudes and patterns of relating. She determined in her mind that her attitudes and physical behaviors would be healthier in her current relationship. She read Christian books on setting godlier boundaries and had long talks about this with Bill.

Spoke #4: Social

I remember a client who called and asked if he could bring his girlfriend along for a counseling session. I asked him how long he'd been seeing this girl. He replied, "Three weeks." I immediately responded that meeting his therapist was far too intimate for only the third week of a new relationship (I also told him I hoped he hadn't introduced her to his mom yet, either). Instant intimacy would be nice, but bypassing the social process of getting to know someone over time isn't wise.

On the other hand, as Christian counselors we also become concerned when *social intimacy* lags behind physical intimacy. When a couple doesn't have enough social intimacy to be comfortable passing gas together but is sexually active, something's wrong. Bill and Tina were well served by their community as they shared fellowship with mature Christians, learning biblical principles for phileo and agape love (Colossians 3:12–14; 1 Corinthians 13:4–7). They appreciated the wonderful models of transparent and caring companionship they were able to observe as they worked on their social intimacy.

Spoke #5: Physical

God created humans with bodies that can express the desires and feelings of the soul. *Physical intimacy* involves much more than just erotic touch. Lovetouching (chapter 14) is an important part of expressing intimacy in Coupling. Yet non-erotic touches, hugs, and shoulder rubs also develop physical intimacy.

Three levels of sensual zones exist in the body, and all can be erogenous (that is, erotically stimulating). The lighter *level three* zone is the skin of the entire body, which is obviously sensitive to touch. *Level two* zones have greater numbers of nerve endings or are near the primary erogenous zones of the genitals or nipples. Level two zones include the mouth, neck, tummy, inner thighs, backs of the knees, lower back, and most places on the head. *Level one* zones are the genital areas of the penis and clitoris, which are capable of stimulation to create orgasms (beware that some level two zones can stimulate orgasm for certain people too).

As previously stated, the "bikini line" stop sign helps protect mutual orgasms, preserving what should be enjoyed only in the covenant of marriage. But because all humans need physical affirmation, physical intimacy can be developed generously in connecting relationships through level three hugs, pats on the back and shoulders, and non-erotic caresses of the arm. Those in Coupling should prayerfully consider which level two zones are safe for enjoyment while still guarding against true sex.

Tina found she had difficulty separating past romantic experiences (with poor physical boundaries) from her present love for Bill. After talking it through, they decided on what some would consider rather conservative stop signs. But for Bill and Tina, these boundaries gave them freedom to develop greater intimacy along the other four spokes while providing a healing experience for Tina.

Stop Signs: Growing and Protecting Intimacy

Implementing healthy boundaries into Coupling takes time, prayerful consideration, and lots of honest dialogue. However, it's well worth the investment. Mutually discuss and choose helpful stop signs for all five spokes in each type of relationship. Remember that stop signs are behaviors you choose by an act of your will not to engage in until you've crossed over into the next stage of your relationship.

Creating Stop Signs

Copy the following chart, filling in the stop signs you want to post in your relationship. Posting a stop sign will mean delaying the intimacy of that particular experience until a future stage, as determined by each couple. You may want to refer back to the three-step inside-out process discussed in chapter 14 for help creating your stop signs. We can't overemphasize the importance of making intentional decisions *ahead of time*. The heat of the moment (1:00 a.m. in her apartment) is a terrible time for trying to think rationally. It simply won't work. Such decisions often result in irreparable damage to the relationship.

		Spiritual	Emotional	Mental	Social	Physical
Connecting	Friendship					
	Considering					
Coupling	Considering					
	Confirming					
	Committing					
Covenanting	Marriage					

Examples of Stop Signs

The same stop sign might fit under more than one spoke of developing intimacy. For example, visiting your old neighborhood or reliving your childhood experiences could fit under both emotional and social. Here are but a few examples to see how intimacy in each area might be established or protected:

Spiritual: Having a deep theological discussion about spiritual topics you might take personally (e.g., speaking in tongues, predestination); praying together after midnight; participating in private worship together alone; visiting a place in nature you consider a "spiritual sanctuary"

Social: Introducing your partner to parents, children (for those single-again), or your "inner-circle" relationships; going to a friend's wedding; inviting your partner to attend your church (especially if it's small); seeing each other daily

193

Emotional: Choosing to disclose your childhood abuse and its effects on you; saying "I love you"; sharing certain movies together; crying in each other's arms; revealing personal fears

Mental: Discussing sensitive topics (politics, child rearing philosophy, etc.); talking about STDs or other personal topics; sharing future goals and dreams; engaging in some types of verbal sexual bantering

Physical: Limiting specific physical expressions of affection, such as kissing only after the confirming stage; refraining from erotic behaviors after a romantic movie or after midnight; limiting private time alone; having sexual discussions in a public place; reserving enjoyment within the bikini line for marriage

The Hazard of Rolling Stops

Remember, merely posting a stop sign isn't enough (though it's a good start). You must also choose to obey your stop sign. It will accomplish nothing if you're going to treat it as a *rolling stop*. You've got to apply the brakes *before* you get to your posted stop sign. Otherwise, you'll find yourself sitting in the middle of the intersection by the time you actually come to a complete stop.

Here's a helpful illustration I (Michael Todd) sometimes use with singles. Let's say while driving you approach an intersection where a crossing guard is escorting a group of children across the street. He or she is holding a stop sign, and as you get closer, you realize the guard is someone you recognize—your coupling partner! At what point would you choose to apply the brakes?

I bet you'd hit those brakes *long before* you actually got to that intersection. Coasting through the stop and gradually slowing down thereafter would result in not only injury to the one you love but also harm to potentially dozens of others.

This example illustrates the importance of respecting posted stop signs in your relationship. You established them for good reason. It's also a reminder that your partner isn't the only one who may suffer when you roll through stop signs. Others may also be harmed in the process, such as friends who hear of your mistake—not to mention your partner's future spouse. Regardless, the bottom line is to respect a stop sign as a "stop" and not as a gradual rolling slowdown.

"Take Good Care of Her—She's a Lease"

As in the real world, stop signs won't keep you safe if you disregard them. Godly Coupling takes hard work—lots more than simply throwing caution to the wind and "letting what happens happen." *But soul virgins are intentional from their hearts in obeying posted stop signs.* They also practice good relational "car care," not only in maintaining tire balance but also in keeping up the overall integrity of the relational vehicle. Nurturing a love relationship with God, enjoying intimate friendships, and living fully as a single adult all contribute to good maintenance.

You don't want to run your relational vehicle into the ground so it becomes no better than an old jalopy. After all, a time in life comes for all of us when our lease expires and the vehicle has to be returned to God, its rightful Owner. On that day, you will have to account for your care of it. Wise stewardship now will prevent extreme penalties when the lease comes due—whether it's next month due to a breakup or after a lifetime of enjoyment and commitment.

Regardless of where you are as a Christian single along the Relationship Continuum Bridge, being content with where you are in your journey is key (Philippians 4:12–13). Balanced intimacy and sexual wholeness will certainly help. Don't be so eager for what you don't have that you're unable to enjoy the benefits of your current relational status. Whether widowed, single-again, or never-married, each single person can learn to savor his or her singleness. Perhaps it's an acquired taste for some, but the single-adult cookie jar has been filled to the brim just for you.

Conclusion

Sixteen
The Cookie Jar

Treats for Singles
with David Hall

Principle:
Savor the richness of single adulthood

Jenny enjoyed being back with family around the holidays. Of course, she had her own place in a different city, but her parents' house always felt like home. But now she was in her late twenties, and her aunts would comment loud enough for her to hear, "How is such a sociable and beautiful girl still single?" They thought surely she must be doing something wrong. Their remarks would irritate her occasionally, but she shrugged them off with a smile. They simply didn't understand.

Jenny loved her job up north. It wasn't really a career, but it was fulfilling, and she had all the money she needed for now. Her job allowed her to travel to many interesting places. Many of her friends were also still single. They were a great supportive network, spending time together that many of their married friends no longer had.

In spite of what her family thought, Jenny hoped to marry one day. She believed God was preparing her for her very own Adam. Singleness did have its difficult moments—she knew them well. Some nights her pillow wasn't enough. She wanted a man in bed to cuddle with and to make her feel special. And at the end of their "girls' nights out," she was a bit envious that her married friends were going home to their loving husbands.

For the most part, however, she had made peace with this sexual ache. Her male friends understood that sometimes she needed an extra-long hug or someone just to tell her she looked pretty. She was thankful for these brothers and prayed her future Adam was equally cared for by the women in his life.

Jenny didn't resent her singleness and knew part of her would mourn when she might someday have to let it go. She could righteously flirt with her dad and brother and play with her young cousins without worrying about neglecting her husband's needs. Her time was truly her own. But her favorite part of being back home was the cookie jar.

Her grandmother's Christmas cookies were legendary. But now her married sister Amy wouldn't touch them because of her low-carb regimen. Her brother James was dieting because he could no longer find time to exercise between night school and his full-time job. The cookies were all hers, and Jenny would savor them one by one. They were little treasures which could so easily have been neglected but in which she took the simplest delight. One day she too might not be able to "afford" them. But for this season, they were hers without regret or second thought. The cookie jar was for her.

Enjoying the "Cookies" of Singleness

Let's be honest. If you're a single adult, you probably at times wish you weren't. Though singleness may be an honorable status, most of the world thinks of it as "second class" to marriage. In a culture that caters to couples and a Christian community that often promotes marriage as the blissful state to which everyone should aspire, singles can all too easily become envious of marriage and ignore the many advantages of single adulthood. If you're presently single—whether never married, widowed, or single again—we encourage you to savor the richness of your present singleness.

If we asked singles to list the benefits of having a spouse, they might include having a sex partner, cuddle buddy, friend, provider, encourager, leader, helper, "solution." Well, most wouldn't say "solution," but it's unconsciously there for many singles: "If I had a wife, I wouldn't look at porn because I'd never be bored." "If I had a husband, I wouldn't stay up all hours of the night in Internet chat rooms." "If I had a spouse, I wouldn't be lonely." These "ifs" sometimes paralyze us in our singleness. Marriage becomes a sort of idol we think will fix all our troubles. Consequently, our singleness will either be used as an excuse for not taking responsibility for our current problems or will blind us to the blessings God does bring to our lives. We become unadventurous and uninspired singles, frustrated sexually and otherwise.

Singleness has gifts for the moment that many take for granted. Single guys often don't look forward to the lack of autonomy in marriage: "I won't be able to stay up late and watch the ball game" or "I'll hate having to 'check in' when I'm on a business trip." Singles can spontaneously go to a midnight movie or meet a friend for coffee anytime. They don't have concerns about losing their privacy and having to share a bathroom with a mate. In marriage, pairing up a morning person and a night owl might mean "sleeping in" becomes a thing of the past.

Single adults have the ability to cultivate personal interests and make individual choices in ways marrieds often cannot. Singles enjoy greater financial freedom, with more discretionary income available to invest in education, missions, career, or just plain fun. A young man who wants to spend a month honing his mountain-climbing skills in Katmandu will have an easier time of it as a single. The woman who wants to relocate to take a low-paying cellist position in the big-city orchestra can do so more easily when she doesn't have a husband's job to consider. I (Michael Todd) support two different single women overseas on the mission field. One in particular struggled significantly with her decision to move overseas—torn between staying here to pursue a husband *in resentment of* her singleness and the freedom to uniquely serve God in a foreign country *because of* her singleness. While not easy, learning to embrace her singleness rather than despising it has made all the difference (1 Corinthians 7:32–35).

With married friends, you'll undoubtedly see the compromising that has to be made in Covenanting regarding money, time, mobility, and other matters. Of course, for them the sacrifices are worth the payoff. They are sacrifices one makes to gain the benefits that come with being married. Neither singleness nor married life is "better" than the other—merely different. But as singles, God calls us to wisely steward the freedoms and gifts he has given us. May we never, like the lazy servant (Matthew 25:14–30), bury what we've been entrusted for this season of our lives and not use it to the glory of God.

"I'd Like an Order of Sexuality, Please—Hold the Sex"

The Wendy's restaurant chain ran a commercial in the mid-1980s that popularized the catchphrase, "Where's the beef?" Many of you might be asking a similar question: "Where's the sex?" The benefits of singleness in freedom, finances, and the like might be easier to see. But your sexual surges always seem to be nagging you. Where's the "treat" for that? The answer may be a bit more complicated and the rewards less dramatic than you'd like, but bear with us.

In our culture, sexuality has been reduced to body parts and the buzz of orgasms. And single adults have been cheated because of it. We introduced the concept of God's sexual economy in chapter 2. Perhaps one way to describe the benefits of singleness is to say that single adults get to spend greater time in the "wider spaces" of the outer gift box of sexuality and connecting relationships. Take the Relationship Continuum Bridge, for example. A married couple lives with each other on the Covenanting side of the bridge. They may have a few good relationships on the Connecting side of things (and Coupling, of course, loses all significance), but the priority of their covenanting relationship necessarily takes up the lion's share of their overall energy. Deeper connecting relationships other than with one's spouse become difficult to maintain. This is the reason many singles who marry begin spending less and less time with their single friends. It's not that they no longer care to be around them; it's just their priorities have changed—and rightly so.

On the other hand, singles have the benefit of spending their energy in a greater number of connecting relationships. For single adults, a hug, back rub, compliment, or listening ear from a connecting friend goes a long way toward filling their needs in the larger box of sexuality. Yet these simple affirmations wouldn't always be considered appropriate for a married person to receive from a friend. For singles, this is the time for full enjoyment of "righteous flirting." Though they may long for the deeper fulfillment of true sex in married life, the outer box of sexuality has potential for a wider variety of interactions that wouldn't necessarily be available to anyone but singles.

A Tale of Two Parties

Think about two different ways of eating a meal at a party. Brad, the married man, sits in the small dining room at a formal party. A generous portion of food is brought out on an oversized plate, and he eats until he's content. He sits and talks with the woman across from him and is enchanted with her. They converse the entire evening as he gets to know her intimately. At the end of the night, he's had a delightful time.

Next door to the dining room is a much larger banquet hall. Molly, a single girl, is at this party. It has no sit-down meal or large portions of food, but a huge buffet offers a seemingly endless variety of finger foods. It's more difficult to make a meal of this. But she returns her smaller plate to the buffet table often until she too is content.

Some singles can be seen sitting in the corner of the banquet hall sulking about not being in the dining room at the formal dinner party. Yet Molly enjoys the variety of cuisines and moves about the room freely, talking to different people with each trip to the buffet. Some are old friends, some are newer friends, and some she's just met for the first time. At the end of the night, she has had a wonderful time. If she chooses to go out for a cup of coffee to extend the evening, no permission is needed. She won't be concerned about what others think of her spending time in great conversation with a man until the coffee shop closes after midnight. It's part of the freedom that comes with her singleness.

Both the formal and the banquet were great parties. They were different from each other, each with their unique benefits and drawbacks. To see one as inferior to the other would be shortsighted. Singles may long for the day they are invited to the exclusive party in the dining room, while their married friends may long for a return to the freedoms of the banquet hall. Rather than focusing on what is not, each should take pleasure in their own party. The apostle Paul (himself a lifelong single adult) gave much the same advice: "I wish everyone could get along without marrying, just as I do. But we are not all the same. God gives some the gift of marriage, and to others he gives the *gift of singleness*" (1 Corinthians 7:7 NLT, emphasis added).

A Quiet Honeymoon with Christ

The final benefit of singleness is easiest to overlook, yet it's likely the most important. First Corinthians 7 is filled with the benefits of singleness. As a single adult, you have the ability to serve God more "singularly" and wholeheartedly than the married adult whose interests are necessarily divided.

God pursues you, his bride, in the ultimate dance of desire. No matter how great a human lover you may one day find, none will fill your deepest need for intimacy as Christ can. All people are called to singleness for at least part of their lives. Yet none of us is called to singleness forever.

Some have earthly spouses and some do not. Yet when all is said and done, you *will* be Christ's bride. In the larger love story, all who claim the name of Jesus find themselves "Coupling with Christ," awaiting the grand wedding ceremony where they will be forever with him—enjoying a party of cosmic proportions and a spread featuring new wine from the true Vine and the choicest of fruits from the Tree of Life.

Such a day is coming, dear friends! Until then we are to enjoy what each has been given, whether in the dining room or the banquet hall. Someday all this talk of earthly dining rooms and banquet halls will fade away into the ultimate reality of what our hearts *truly long for*, married and single alike.

As a single for now, dedicate your time in the "wider spaces" by cultivating many interesting friendships around the banquet table—but most importantly, by cultivating a passionate love affair with Christ, the intimate lover of your soul.

Appendix

Here is a list of "conversation starters" for getting to know someone better early in the relationship. Perhaps these will whet your appetite to create some of your own.

- What are your favorite hobbies? Restaurants? Foods? Vacation destinations? Movies? Actors? Sports? Athletes? Books? Authors? Things to talk about?
- What is your favorite style of music? Favorite song? Who are your favorite artists/musicians? What instruments do you play? Wish you played?
- Do you prefer: the beach or the mountains? Diet or regular soda? Spring or Fall? Dining in or out? Movies in or out? Cats or dogs? Paper or plastic?
- Where did you attend high school/college? What did you study?
- Describe your work. What do you like/dislike about it? Is it a career or a "job"?
- Describe your typical week/weekend. What's an ideal week? Weekend?
- Describe your perfect Saturday.
- Describe your church. What groups/studies/ministries are you involved in?
- Where else in the country/world might you want to live? Why?
- Describe your best friends. What do you like most about them? Why?
- Who is the funniest person you know? What makes them funny?
- What makes you smile?
- How would your closest friends describe you? Your personality type?
- What's the most spontaneous thing you've ever done? In the past year?
- What is unique about you?
- Describe your family (parents, siblings, etc.) and where you lived growing up.

- In what ways would you consider yourself traditional? Non-traditional?
- Describe your favorite memories as a child, teenager, or adult. Why are they your favorites?
- Describe your funniest/fondest memories growing up.
- How did (or have) you come to Christ? Describe your walk with the Lord now.
- What causes do you believe in? Volunteer for? Support financially?
- Who has influenced you most and how? Who are your role models? Mentors?
- What would you change about your life if you could? What prevents you?
- What dreams would you follow if you could? Why? What stops you?
- What would you want people to say or remember about you after you're gone?

Notes

Chapter 3: Living Boldly from Your Heart

1. www.WashingtonPost.com/WP-dyn/articles/A48509-2005Mar18.html.

Chapter 5: God's Sexual ER

1. Anonymous, *Sexaholics Anonymous*, new and rev. ed. (SA Literature, 1989), 6, emphasis added.

Chapter 6: One *Is* a Whole Number

1. John Piper, *Desiring God* (Sisters, OR: Multnomah, 2003), 288.

Chapter 7: Soul-Sexy Masculinity

1. John Eldredge, *Wild at Heart* (Nashville: Thomas Nelson, 2002), 10–11.

Chapter 8: Soul-Sexy Femininity

1. *Webster's Ninth New Collegiate Dictionary*, s.v. *modesty*.
2. Wendy Shallit, *Return to Modesty* (New York: Free Press, 1999), 173.
3. John and Stasi Eldredge, *Captivating* (Nashville: Thomas Nelson, 2005), 25.

Chapter 9: So . . . What *Do* I Do with My Sexual Surging?

1. Paula Rinehart, *Sex and the Soul of a Woman* (Grand Rapids: Zondervan, 2004), 148.

Chapter 10: The Dance of Desire

1. Walter Trobisch, *I Loved a Girl* (Bolivar, MO: Quiet Waters, 2001), 75 76.

Chapter 11: Guy-Girl Connecting

1. Tracey Casale, *Saved for My Beloved: Love Letters to My Future Spouse* (unpublished manuscript). Used with author's permission.

About the Authors

Doug Rosenau, Ed.D., is a licensed psychologist, marriage and family therapist, and Certified Christian Sex Therapist with the American Board of Christian Sex Therapists (ABCST). A pioneer in Christian sex therapy, Dr. Rosenau is author of the best-selling book *A Celebration of Sex*. He is also author of *A Celebration of Sex for Newlyweds* and co-author of *A Celebration of Sex after 50*. Dr. Rosenau is a graduate of Dallas Theological Seminary (Th.M.) and received his doctorate in counseling (Ed.D.) from Northern Illinois University.

Dr. Rosenau maintains a full clinical practice with the Intimacy Counseling Center in Suwanee, Georgia (Atlanta area). He teaches Human Sexuality and Sex Therapy nationally as a popular conference speaker and as adjunct professor at Richmont Graduate University, Reformed Theological Seminary, and Dallas Theological Seminary. As co-founder of the Christian organization Sexual Wholeness (.com), Doug helped create the Institute for Sexual Wholeness that trains Christian sex therapists and educators.

Dr. Rosenau and his wife, Catherine, live in the Atlanta area. They have a daughter, Merrill, and a granddaughter, Caitlyn, who is the apple of his eye. Doug and Catherine enjoy antiquing and weekends at their cabin in the North Georgia mountains.

http://SexualWholeness.com

Michael Todd Wilson, M.S., is a licensed professional counselor, life coach, and Certified Christian Sex Therapist with the American Board of Christian Sex Therapists. Michael Todd earned his graduate degree in counseling (M.S.) from Georgia State University and also attended Psychological Studies Institute, both in Atlanta, Georgia. He has also provided clinical supervision for graduate counseling students at both Reformed Theological Seminary and Psychological Studies Institute.

In addition to clinical practice with Doug at the Intimacy Counseling Center, Michael Todd is director and cofounder of ShepherdCare, a nonprofit ministry dedicated to helping those in pastoral ministry avoid burnout and moral failure by practicing healthy self-care through conferences and related services.

Michael Todd is a never-married single adult and lives in the Atlanta area. He enjoys playing board games, golfing with his dad, and daydreaming about driving on the Indianapolis Motor Speedway.

Want to Experience More Soul Virginity?

Check out these additional resources to further your *Soul Virgin* journey:

Soul Virgins Website (www.SoulVirgins.com)—A clearinghouse for single adults related to the area of sexuality. The site contains up-to-date information on new projects from Doug and Michael Todd, Soul Virgin event schedules, related articles, and links to other websites of interest for the Christian single.

A Celebration of Sex for Newlyweds—An excellent resource from best-selling author Doug Rosenau containing all the information a couple approaching marriage will want to know and discuss together, from enjoying lovemaking cycles to minimizing the mess to maximizing the honeymoon (available now from your local Christian retailer).

Soul Virgin Singles Events—Interested in having Doug and Michael Todd come to your church or singles group for a Soul Virgins event or retreat? Contact them through the Soul Virgins website.

Coaching toward Greater Soul Virginity—Want to work directly with the authors to implement soul virginity into your own connecting and coupling relationships? Michael Todd offers individual and group coaching via telephone. Coaching can be an effective way to personalize and integrate this material into your unique relationships. Contact Michael Todd through the Soul Virgins website or through his personal website, www.MichaelToddWilson.com.

Praise...

"Singles are often told to simply 'wait,' but rarely does anyone fully explain why or how. With great wisdom and remarkable insight, Rosenau and Wilson escort singles into a much fuller understanding not just of how to postpone sex, but of the beautiful gift that God has woven into the fibers of their being —their sexuality. This is a must-read for Christian singles!"

Shannon Ethridge, coauthor,
Every Young Woman's Battle

"It's rare to find a book with content that is new and original but this long-overdue book is just that. Doug and Michael help us see that sex is about a whole lot more than merely doing 'it.' Sex and sexuality are about intimacy with God and others that includes our body, soul, and spirit. It's realistic and practical and answers the most delicate and difficult questions in ways that are honest and make sense. This book will make you laugh, make you think, make you squirm, challenge some of your assumptions, and with some application bring a smile to your face and greater joy and fulfillment to your relationships. I guarantee that this is a book you will want to read more than once."

Gary J. Oliver, executive director,
Center for Relationship Development
at John Brown University

"A freeing book on single sexuality, *Soul Virgins* combines biblical wisdom with grace and humor. Single adults will appreciate the frankness and personal relevance the authors bring to this crucial topic."

Greg Smalley, coauthor, *The DNA of Relationships*,
professor, Center for Relationship Development
at John Brown University

"Having ministered for years to single people who struggle with living out their sexuality in God-pleasing ways—and having seen so many fail—I know that new approaches are needed. *Soul Virgins: Redefining Single Sexuality* offers an exciting new approach, one that is realistic, challenging, and even a bit scary—but one that I believe can work for many people."

Alan Medinger, author, *Growth Into Manhood*;
executive director, Regeneration

"Whether you have done it all right or messed up big time, this book will pour hope, healing, and vital information into you and enable you to view your sexuality in a totally new way! We highly recommend *Soul Virgins!*"

Linda Dillow and Lorraine Pintus, co-authors of
Giftwrapped by God and *Intimate Issues*

Made in the USA
Middletown, DE
12 December 2020

27233975R00130